C000145755

COMBAT
AIRCRAFT
RECOGNITION

3rd Edition

PETER R. MARCH

ZH588

PLYMOUTH PRESS

Ian Allan
PUBLISHING

First published 1988
Second edition 1992
Third edition 1998

ISBN 0 7110 2590 8

© Ian Allan Ltd 1998

Published by Ian Allan Publishing
an imprint of Ian Allan Publishing Ltd, Terminal House, Station Approach, Shepperton, Surrey TW17 8AS.
Printed by Ian Allan Printing Ltd at its works at Riverdene Business Park, Molesey Road, Hersham, Surrey, KT12 4RG

Code: 9806/C2

Front cover: BAe Sea Harrier FA2 in service with the Royal Navy. *PRM*

Above: USAF Lockheed C-130H Hercules, the workhorse of the Worlds' air arms. *PRM*

Title page: Eurofighter Typhoon is expected to enter service with the RAF, German, Italian and Spanish Air Forces. *PRM BAe*

Below: Westland Sea Kings serve with both the RAF and Royal Navy.. *PRM*

Contents

Acknowledgements

The author would like to thank Ben Dunnell and Brian Strickland for the detailed research and preparation of the material.

Photographs

Most of the copyright illustrations in *abc Combat Aircraft Recognition* are from the PRM Aviation Photo Library as follows: Andrew P. March (APM), Daniel J. March (DJM) and Peter R. March (PRM). Additional photographs as credited.

Peter R. March is also author of the following publications:

abc Military Aircraft Markings, Ian Allan Ltd, 1998
abc Light Aircraft Recognition, Ian Allan Ltd, 1997
abc Civil Airliner Recognition, Ian Allan Ltd, 1997
abc Classic & Warbird Recognition, Ian Allan Ltd, 1996
abc Biz Jets, Ian Allan Ltd, 1996
Confederate Air Force — Celebrating 40 years, CAF, 1997; Sabre to Stealth, RAFBFE, 1997;
Hawk Comes of Age, RAFBFE, 1995;
The Real Aviation Enthusiast II, RAFBFE, 1995;
Royal Air Force Almanac, RAFBFE, 1994;
and is Managing Editor of the Royal Air Force Yearbook and USAF Yearbook series (RAF Benevolent Fund Enterprises).

Introduction

This revised third edition of *abc Combat Aircraft Recognition* has been produced in series with *abc Classic & Warbird Recognition*, *abc Light Aircraft Recognition* and *abc Civil Airliner Recognition*, and is a companion to *abc Military Aircraft Markings* and *abc UK Military Airfields*. *abc Combat Aircraft Recognition* brings together in one full-colour publication a compact guide to the military aircraft that are likely to be seen in the skies of the western world. Many of the types described are in front-line service with NATO, European and former Warsaw Pact countries and on this basis fully justify the description 'modern combat aircraft'. Other aircraft like the BAe Hawk fill an operational training role in peacetime, but some can be armed with Sidewinder missiles to assume a front-line tasking in the event of a threat to peace. Similarly, there are many other transport and training fixed-wing types and helicopters that provide combat support as trainers, freight and passenger carriers, medical evacuation, reconnaissance, airborne early warning, maritime surveillance and aerial tanking roles, that would be drawn more closely into front-line operations.

The abc provides a guide to the fascinating variety of combat aircraft likely to be seen at military airfields, airshows and flying through our skies. All of the major types are presented in the established abc 'Recognition Series' format. It contains basic technical information on one of the variants, the date that the first aircraft (usually the prototype) was flown, when it first entered military service, production details and an indication of the air arms using this aircraft, either currently or in recent years. Details of the armament normally carried or the accommodation for crew/passengers and/or cargo are quoted where applicable. The main recognition features are listed and where there are several variants these are also noted. Colour photographs are used to aid recognition, and distinctive variants are also illustrated where possible.

The second section provides a brief guide to some of the older combat aircraft that are seeing their final days of service, together with some of the support aircraft that are in service in relatively small numbers.

Performance Abbreviations

ehp	equivalent horsepower	shp	shaft horsepower
kN	kilonewton	eshp	equivalent shaft horsepower
kW	kilowatt	st	static thrust
hp	horsepower	mph	miles per hour
		km/h	kilometres per hour

Aermacchi MB-339

**Single-turbojet two-seat advanced trainer
and light-attack aircraft**
Basic data for MB-339A
Powerplant: One Rolls-Royce Viper 632-43
turbojet of 4,000lb st (17.79kN)
Span: 35ft 5in (10.80m)
Length: 36ft 0in (10.97m)
Max speed: 558mph (899km/h)
Armament: Up to 4,500lb (2,040kg) of external
stores on six hardpoints, including bombs,
rockets, cannon pods and Matra anti-shipping
missiles.
First aircraft flown: 12 August 1976
Entered service: 8 August 1978
Current service: With the Italian AF and the air
arms of Argentina, Dubai, Ghana, Malaysia, New
Zealand, Nigeria and Peru.
Recognition: Low-set wings with a slightly swept
leading-edge, normally fitted with wingtip fuel
tanks. Small oval air intakes are located at the
wing roots and a single jetpipe extends beyond
the fin and tailplane. Vertical and horizontal tail
surfaces are small and angular. The single-place
cockpit (MB-339K) and the longer tandem

cockpit (MB-339A) are set forward of the wing. A
more streamlined nose and cockpit largely
differentiates the MB-339 from the earlier MB-
326.
Variants: MB-339A built as a two-seat trainer.
The MB-339K (first flown on 30 May 1980, but
which has not seen production) and the MB-339B
are armed versions with the more powerful Rolls-
Royce Viper 680-43 turbojet. The trainer/attack
MB-339C, first flown on 17 December 1985, is
also fitted with the uprated Rolls-Royce Viper 680-
43 and equipped to carry air-to-air and air-to-
surface missiles. Latest and most advanced of the
derivatives is the MB-339FD (Full Digital) — this
entered Italian AF service as the MB-339CD in
1997.

Below: **The Aermacchi MB-339 advanced
trainer and light-attack aircraft entered
service in 1978.** *PRM*

Aero L-39/L-59 Albatros

Single-turbofan two-seat advanced trainer

Basic data for L-39ZO

Powerplant: One Ivchenko AI-25TL turbofan of 3,792lb st (16.87kN)

Span: 31ft 5in (9.46m)

Length: 39ft 9½in (12.13m)

Max speed: 466mph (755km/h)

Armament: The L-39ZO has four underwing hardpoints; the L-39ZA adds an underfuselage gun pod. Up to 6,000lb of stores can be carried by the new L-159.

First aircraft flown: 4 November 1968

Entered service: 1974

Current service: Over 2,000 with the air arms of Afghanistan, Algeria, Bulgaria, Congo, Cuba, Czech Republic, Egypt, Ethiopia, Hungary, Iraq, Kazakhstan, Libya, Lithuania, Nicaragua, Nigeria, North Korea, Russia, Slovakia, Syria, Thailand and Vietnam.

Recognition: Slim fuselage with long tandem cockpit canopy. Very long nose and short-span unswept wings, with tip tanks, which are set low on the fuselage. Engine intakes are positioned in the upper fuselage sides behind the cockpit for the internally mounted engine. Tailplane is set high on the fuselage at rear base of fin.

Variants: As successor to the L-29 Delfin, the L-39 Albatros was selected as the standard jet trainer of all the Warsaw Pact countries (except Poland). The standard aircraft was developed into the basic L-39C basic and advanced trainer, the L-39ZO weapons trainer, the L-39ZA ground-attack and reconnaissance version and the L-39V target tug. The updated L-39MS (designated L-59 for export) has more powerful engines and improved avionics, while the projected L-139 is intended to use a US engine. First flown on 2 August 1997, the single-seat L-159 (powered by the F124 turbofan) has been ordered for the light attack role by the Czech AF.

Below: **This Czech L-39 Albatros has been operated by more than a dozen air arms since 1974.** *PRM / DJM*

Aérospatiale Alouette II/III

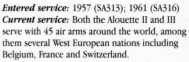

Single-turboshaft multi-role helicopter
Basic data for SA316B Alouette III
Powerplant: One Turboméca Artouste IIIB turboshaft of 570eshp (425kW)
Rotor diameter: 36ft 1¼in (11.02m)
Fuselage length: 32ft 11in (10.04m)
Max speed: 130mph (210km/h)
Armament: Variety of external weapons including AS11 anti-tank missiles or two Mk 44 torpedoes.
Accommodation: Two crew plus up to six passengers or cargo
First aircraft flown: 12 March 1955 (SA313B); 28 February 1959 (SA316)

Entered service: 1957 (SA313); 1961 (SA316)
Current service: Both the Alouette II and III serve with 45 air arms around the world, among them several West European nations including Belgium, France and Switzerland.
Recognition: Alouette II has a skeletal rear fuselage with a three-blade tail rotor. The cabin section is glazed on all sides except the floor. The externally mounted turboshaft is uncowled and mounted to the rear of the main single-rotor driveshaft. A skid undercarriage is standard. The Alouette III has a fully covered frame with a larger less-glazed cabin. A fixed tricycle undercarriage has external bracing to the rear of the cabin section.
Variants: The initial production Alouette II was replaced or supplemented by the more powerful Astazou-engined SA315 Lama, SA318C, and the larger SA316/319 Alouette III. HAL of India continues to licence-build the Alouette III as the Chetak, and it was produced in Romania by ICA-Brasov until 1989.

Above: **The earlier Alouette II has a narrower cockpit section.** *PRM*

Below: **An Aérospatiale Alouette III in Swiss Army colours.** *PRM*

Aérospatiale (Sud) SA321 Super Frelon

Three-turboshaft heavy ASW and utility helicopter
Basic data for SA321G
Powerplant: Three Turboméca Turmo IIIC6 turboshafts of 1,630eshp (1,215kW)
Rotor diameter: 62ft 0in (18.90m)
Fuselage length: 63ft 7¾in (19.40m)
Max speed: 171mph (275km/h)
Accommodation: Up to 30 troops or 8,818lb payload (internal) or 11,023lb payload (external)
First aircraft flown: 7 December 1962
Entered service: 1965
Current service: With the French Navy (SA321G), Argentina, Iraq and Libya (SA321H), China (SA321J)
Recognition: Single six-blade main rotor above a bulbous fuselage with an extended tail boom and five-blade tail rotor on the port side. Engines mounted above the cabin with front intakes. Boat hull underside with floats (most versions) outboard of the fixed undercarriage. Rear loading ramp below tail boom.
Variants: The two main variants are the ASW version with the stabilising floats and anti-submarine equipment, and the utility transport without the floats and ASW fitments. French production ceased in 1983, but Changhi in China continues to licence-build the multi-role Y-8 development.

Above and below: The Aérospatiale SA321 Super Frelon, the French Navy's long-range anti-submarine helicopter. *PRM*

Aérospatiale (SOCATA) TB30 Epsilon

Single-piston-engined two-seat primary trainer and light attack aircraft
Basic data for TB30B
Powerplant: One Textron Lycoming AEIO-540-L1B5D piston engine of 300hp (225kW)
Span: 25ft 11½in (7.92m)
Length: 24ft 10½in (7.59m)
Max speed: 230mph (370km/h)
Armament: Four underwing hardpoints for a variety of stores of up to 661lb (300kg), on Togolese aircraft only
First aircraft flown: 22 December 1979
Entered service: July 1983
Current service: With the French, Portuguese and Togo air forces
Recognition: Low wing of narrow chord set below

Above: Aérospatiale TB30 Epsilon, in service with the French Air Force as a basic trainer, is also available in a ground attack version. *PRM*

the slender fuselage. Two-seat tandem cockpit with a 'glasshouse' canopy. Tall fin and rudder with a similarly shaped tailplane set on the rear fuselage. A distinctive long ventral fin.
Variants: The only other version is the TB31 Omega, powered by a Turboméca Arrius turboprop and first flown on 19 November 1985, but which has remained as a prototype only.

Aérospatiale/Westland SA330 Puma

Twin-turboshaft multi-role helicopter
Basic data for SA330L
Powerplant: Two Turboméca Turmo IVC turboshafts of 1,575eshp (1,175kW)
Rotor diameter: 49ft 2½in (15.00m)
Fuselage length: 46ft 1½in (14.06m)
Max speed: 163mph (263km/h)
Accommodation: Up to 20 passengers/troops or 7,055lb underslung load
First aircraft flown: 15 April 1965
Entered service: June 1970
Current service: With the air arms of many countries including Abu Dhabi, Argentina, Cameroon, Chile, Democratic Republic of Congo, Ecuador, France, Indonesia, Kuwait, Nepal, Nigeria, Portugal and Spain. The RAF uses the Westland-built Puma.
Recognition: Tall, narrow cabin with a deep tail boom. Engines mounted above the cabin, forward of the main rotor hub. Some versions (including RAF Pumas) have extended engine intakes projecting well forward above the windscreen. Large sliding cabin doors; retractable undercarriage, with the main wheels housed in small sponsons. Four-blade main rotor and tail rotor mounted on the starboard side.

Variants: The Aérospatiale SA330 and Westland Puma differ only in detail, being used primarily for Army support, carrying troops and underslung loads. The French Army uses the SA330B, roughly equivalent to the RAF's Puma HC1s; the SA330C was the initial export variant, used for various tasks by numerous air arms.

Above and below: **Aérospatiale SA330 Pumas are in service with 14 air arms.** *APM*

Aérospatiale/Westland SA341, Eurocopter SA342 Gazelle

Light utility and anti-tank helicopter
Basic data for SA341
Powerplant: One Turboméca Astazou XIVM turboshaft of 859eshp (640kW)
Rotor diameter: 34ft 5½in (10.50m)
Fuselage length: 31ft 3¼in (9.53m)
Max speed: 193mph (310km/h)
Armament: Two 7.62mm machine guns or 20mm GIAT cannon, plus four or six HOT or AS11 anti-armour missiles, or rocket pods. French Army SA341/342s have four Mistral infra-red homing missiles.
First aircraft flown: 7 April 1967 (France); 6 August 1971 (UK)
Entered service: 1969 (France); 1972 (UK)
Current service: With the UK Army Air Corps and Royal Marines (AH1), French Army (SA341F/SA342), China, Croatia, Egypt, Iraq, Kuwait, Libya and several other air arms worldwide.

Recognition: Tadpole-shaped fuselage with the front section fully glazed. Distinctive fenestron (enclosed) tail rotor with a small tailplane just forward of it, with end plates. The engine is mounted behind and above the cabin with the jetpipe extending over the start of the tailboom. Missile-equipped variants have a stabilised sight above the cabin.
Variants: The SA341 and SA342 are similar in external appearance; the differences are in engine power, a strengthened fenestron and avionics. Westland-built Gazelles for the British services have some minor equipment differences. Eurocopter France's most recent production versions are the SA342L (export) and the SA342M (French Army).

Below: **Westland Gazelle AH1s remain in service with the Army Air Corps.** *PRM*

Agusta A109

Twin-turboshaft multi-role light utility and anti-tank helicopter
Basic data for A109KM
Powerplant: Two Turboméca Arriel 1K1 turboshafts of 632eshp (471kW)
Rotor diameter: 36ft 1in (11.00m)
Fuselage length: 37ft 6in (11.44m)
Max speed: 193mph (311km/h)
Armament: Eight HeliTOW 2 missiles, Stinger A 7.62mm or 12.7mm machine guns, rocket launchers and ASW equipment; weapons carried on two pylon-mounted external hardpoints on each side of the fuselage.
First aircraft flown: 4 August 1971
Entered service: 1977
Current service: With the Italian Army (primarily the A109EOA), Argentina, Belgium (the A109BA), Greece, Malaysia, Morocco, Saudi Arabia, Singapore, Slovenia, UK and Venezuela.
Recognition: Streamlined front fuselage and a tapered rear boom with a twin-blade tail rotor. The engines are enclosed above the cabin with a four-blade main rotor. The tricycle undercarriage retracts into the fuselage. As well as a conventional fin, the A109 has a distinctive ventral fin.
Variants: A109C — executive/corporate helicopter; A109CM — multi-role military version; A109G di F — coastguard variant operated by Italy; A109K2 — optimised for hot-and-high multi-purpose operations; A109KM — the military version developed for military operations; A109 Power — the latest version, with improved avionics (yet to be ordered for military service).

Above and below: **The Agusta A109A is a light utility and anti-tank helicopter.** *Andy Martin / PRM*

Agusta A129 Mangusta

Twin-turboshaft attack and scout helicopter

Basic data for A129

Powerplant: Two Rolls-Royce Gem 2-1004D turboshafts of 825eshp (615kW)

Rotor diameter: 39ft ½in (11.90m)

Fuselage length: 40ft 3¼in (12.17m)

Max speed: 161mph (259km/h)

Armament: Eight TOW missiles plus machine gun up to 20mm or two air-to-surface rocket launchers with seven rockets in each; also 7.62mm, 12.7mm or 20mm gun pods. Additionally, armament can include Stinger, Hellfire or Mistral ASMs, or Sidewinder AAMs.

First aircraft flown: 11 September 1983 (A129); 9 January 1995 (A129 International)

Entered service: October 1990

Current service:
Only with the Italian Army

Recognition: Narrow slab-sided fuselage with two separate cockpits, the second being behind and above and forward of the enclosed engines. Fixed tailwheel undercarriage, the rear wheel beneath the ventral tailfin. A large swept fin and tailplanes set on the fuselage sides. Armament carried on stub wings high on the mid-fuselage sides below the engine intakes.

Variants: A129 International has two LHTEC (Allison/AlliedSignal) T800-LHT-800 turboshafts of 1,335shp (996kW) with a five-blade main rotor. Weaponry options include Stinger ASMs, a Lockheed Martin/GIAT 20mm three-barrelled cannon, FLIR and CCD displays.

Below: The Agusta A129 Mangusta entered service with the Italian Army in October 1990. *PRM*

Airtech (CASA/IPTN) CN-235

Twin-turboprop military and civil transport

Basic data for CN-235M

Powerplant: Two General Electric CTT-9C turboprops of 1,750eshp (1,305kW)

Span: 84ft 8in (25.81m)

Length: 70ft 2½in (21.40m)

Max cruising speed: 281mph (453.2km/h)

Armament: Three attachment points under each wing. Weapons on the MPA version can include McDonnell Douglas Harpoon or AM39 Exocet anti-ship missiles, or two Mk 46 torpedoes. Accommodation: As transport can accommodate 48 equipped troops or 46 paratroopers. Flight crew of two, plus loadmaster.

First aircraft flown: 11 November 1983 (CASA); 30 December 1983 (IPTN)

Entered service: 1 March 1988

Current service: Over 175 in service with the air forces of Botswana, Brunei, Chile, Colombia, Ecuador, Eire, France, Gabon, Indonesia, South Korea, Morocco, Panama, Papua New Guinea, Saudi Arabia, Spain, Turkey and UAE.

Recognition: High-mounted wing with no dihedral. Constant-chord centre section. Flattened circular cross-section fuselage with upswept rear end incorporating cargo ramp/door. Sweptback fin and rudder. Low-set non-swept tailplane. Two small ventral fins. Two fairings under fuselage to house main undercarriage. Twin turboprops mounted forward and under leading-edge of wings and a humped bulge at wing roots. Each main landing gear comprises two wheels in tandem and main wheels semi-exposed when retracted.

Variants: Series 100 — original civil version; Series 200 — improved civil version certified 1992; CN-235M — military transport version; CN-235MP and CN-235MPA Persuader — maritime patrol version, with Litton APS-504 search radar and FLIR and ESM. The stretched CN-195 was launched in late 1997.

Below: **The Airtech CN-235 is in service as a medium range transport and maritime patrol aircraft.** *DJM*

Alenia G222

Twin-turboprop tactical transport
Basic data for G222TCM
Powerplant: Two General Electric T64-P4D turboprops of 3,400eshp (2,535kW)
Span: 94ft 2in (28.70m)
Length: 74ft 5½in (22.70m)
Max speed: 303mph (487km/h)
Accommodation: Three/four crew and 53 fully-equipped troops, 42 paratroops or 36 stretchers; a total of 19,841lb (9,000kg) cargo can be carried.
First aircraft flown: 18 July 1970
Entered service: March 1976
Current service: In addition to the Italian AF the G222 serves with the air arms of Argentina, Dubai, Libya, Nigeria, Somalia, Thailand, USA and Venezuela.
Recognition: Long, squat, circular fuselage with a high-set wing which has a narrow chord and no sweep. The powerplants are carried under the wings near to the fuselage. The nose is short and rounded and has a large cockpit with rectangular windows. There are four small circular windows along the sides of the fuselage. The rear part of the body sweeps upwards and includes clamshell doors. The tailfin extends forward with a dorsal section.

Variants: The standard transport as used by the Italian AF is the G222TCM. Specialised versions are designated according to their role, but are externally similar in appearance: G222AA — firefighting; G222RM — radio/radar calibrations; G222M — electronic countermeasures; G222VS — maritime surveillance. In 1990, the type was ordered by the USAF as the C-27A Spartan, 10 being based in Panama for operations in South America.

Below: **An Alenia G222, serving with the RSV of the Italian Air Force.** *PRM*

AMX International AMX

Single-turbofan single-seat tactical strike fighter

Basic data for AMX

Powerplant: One Rolls-Royce Spey Mk 807 turbofan of 11,030lb st (49.1kN)

Span: 29ft 1in (8.87m)

Length: 44ft 7in (13.58m)

Max speed: 567mph (915km/h)

Armament: One 20mm six-barrel General Electric M61A1 Vulcan cannon on Italian aircraft. Two 30mm DEFA 554 cannon on the Brazilian machines. External weapons of up to 8,375lb (3,800kg) on four underwing, one centre line and two wingtip stations. Armaments include AIM-9L Sidewinders and MAA-1 Piranha AAMs on wingtip rails, unguided bombs, rockets and cluster munitions.

First aircraft flown: May 1984; first production aircraft 11 May 1988

Entered service: April 1989

Current service: Air forces of Brazil and Italy

Recognition: Streamlined fuselage with a pronounced bubble canopy. The swept wings are shoulder-mounted on the fuselage. The large rounded intakes for the internally housed turbofan are set at the roots of the wings. The swept tail surfaces are mounted at the rear of the fuselage.

Variants: AMX and A-1 are the Italian and Brazilian single-seaters, used for attack and reconnaissance, with a secondary counter-air role. AMX-T is the two-seat advanced trainer for conversion training and is combat-capable. It is planned to be adopted for ECR and anti-shipping.

Below: **The AMX has been in service with the Italian Air Force since 1989.** *PRM*

Antonov An-24 'Coke'/An-26 'Curl'/An-30 'Clank'

Twin-turboprop short-haul transport aircraft

Basic data for
An-26B 'Curl-B'

Powerplants: Two ZMKB Progress AI-24VT turboprops of 2,780eshp (2,073kW)

Span: 95ft 9½in (29.20m)

Length: 78ft 1in (23.80m)

Max speed: 336mph (540km/h)

Armament: Angolan and Mozambique aircraft have bomb racks

Accommodation: Crew of five. Optional tip-up seats along each wall for total of 38-40 persons. As ambulance, can carry 24 stretcher patients.

First aircraft flown: 21 May 1969

Entered service: Early 1970s

Current service: Over 1,000 built, currently used by the Russian armed forces, those of the former Soviet republics and over 25 export customers.

Recognition: High wing with 2° anhedral on outer panels. Long, slim engine nacelles with conical fairings which protrude beyond wing trailing-edge. Wings of equal taper with square tips. Circular fuselage with dorsal fillet leading to swept fin and rudder. Dihedral swept tailplane set at top of rear fuselage extremity. Twin wheels on all undercarriage legs, which retract forward. 'Beaver-tail' rear fuselage and loading ramp forms underside of rear fuselage.

Variations: An-24 'Coke' — original version that first flew in April 1960; An-26 'Curl-A' — original pressurised version; An-26B 'Curl-A' — improved version introduced in 1981 with additional freight-handling equipment; An-26 'Curl-B' — a signals intelligence (Sigint) version, with many short blade antennae mounted above and below fuselage. The An-30 'Clank', first flown in 1974, is one of the few purpose-designed surveying and mapping aircraft, and has a different forward fuselage with an extended and glazed nose, and raised flightdeck. The An-26 is also produced in China as the Xian YTH-500.

Below: First flown in 1969, the Antonov An-26 is operated in more than 25 countries. *PRM*

BAC VC10

Four-turbofan long-range transport/tanker aircraft

Basic data for VC10 C1K

Powerplant: Four Rolls-Royce Conway 301 turbofans of 21,800lb st (96.97kN)

Span: 146ft 2in (44.55m)

Length: 158ft 8in (48.36m)

Max speed: 581mph (935km/h)

Accommodation: Up to 150 passengers or cargo

First aircraft flown: 29 June 1962

Entered service: 7 July 1966

Current service: With the RAF (10 C1Ks, nine K2/K3s and five K4s)

Recognition: A long circular narrow-body fuselage with low swept wings set well back towards the tail, giving the appearance of having a very long forward fuselage. The pairs of podded engines are mounted on the sides of the rear fuselage below the swept 'T' tail unit. The C1K has a large port-side front freight door; the K2/3 and K4 have underwing podded hose-drum units for in-flight refuelling.

Variants: The VC10 C1K, with its primary transport and secondary tanker roles, has a standard VC10 fuselage with the refinements of the Super VC10. The VC10 K2 is a tanker conversion of the standard airliner while the K3 is a Super VC10 conversion, having a 13ft longer fuselage. The K4s are five additional Super VC10s converted to tankers in the early 1990s, which do not feature main-deck fuel tanks.

Below: **BAC VC10s, converted from civil airliners, provide the majority of the RAF's air refuelling capability.** *PRM*

Beech C-12 Huron/Super King Air

Light twin-turboprop for communications and special duties

Basic data for C-12A/Super King Air 200T
Powerplant: Two Pratt & Whitney PT6A-42 turboprops of 850eshp (635kW)
Span: 54ft 6in (16.60m)
Length: 43ft 9in (13.33m)
Max speed: 262mph (421km/h)
Accommodation: Two crew and up to 13 passengers or cargo
First aircraft flown: 27 October 1972
Entered service: March 1974 with USAF and US Army
Current service: With the USAF, US Army, US Navy, Irish Air Corps, Algeria, Japan, Peru, Sweden, Switzerland and many others in B200 and B350 guises for communications, battlefield support (including electronic reconnaissance) and maritime patrol.

Recognition: Low wing with turboprops projecting well forward of the cockpit. Slender fuselage with near-circular cabin windows high set. Swept fin and rudder with a dorsal extension. The swept tailplane is set high on top of the fin.
Variants: Distinctive variants of the standard Super King Air 200 include the UC-12B/F/M — used by the US Navy, with a large port-side cargo door; the C-12F — operated by the USAF as an operational support aircraft (which followed earlier C-12A/Ds into service); and the RC-12K — a communications and electronic intelligence-gathering platform with the US Army (that operates all C-12 versions). B200s are in service with several nations; the stretched Super King Air 350 is in use by Switzerland, while the C-12J is a Beech 1900 flown by the US Air National Guard as mission support aircraft.

Below: Beech Super King Airs are operated as a communications and special duties aircraft in all the US services. *PRM*

18

Bell AH-1 Cobra/SeaCobra

Single-turboshaft light anti-tank and attack helicopter
Basic data for AH-1S

Powerplant: One Textron Lycoming T53-L-703 turboshaft of 1,800eshp (1,340kW)
Rotor diameter: 44ft 0in (13.41m)
Fuselage length: 44ft 7in (13.59m)
Max speed: 141mph (227km/h)
Armament: 30mm gun or 20mm three-barrel rotary gun; plus eight Hughes TOW anti-tank missiles. Can carry rockets or machine gun pods.
First aircraft flown: 7 September 1965
Entered service: 1967
Current service: With the US Army and Marine Corps; also Bahrain, Egypt, Iran, Israel, Japan, Greece, Jordan, Morocco, Pakistan, South Korea, Thailand and Turkey.
Recognition: Narrow fuselage with a two-seat tandem cockpit. Engine mounted behind the cockpit with a two-blade main rotor above. The tail rotor is mounted at the top of the tailfin. A gun turret is located under the nose, just forward of the main landing skids.
Variants: The AH-1G was produced in large numbers. It has subsequently been replaced by the AH-1S with a modified flat-glass cockpit canopy, new equipment and avionics. Most of the earlier Cobras have been modified to this standard. The main variant that is externally different is the US Marine Corps' AH-1T SeaCobra with a longer fuselage and the General Electric T400 TwinPac engine — these are being converted to the AH-1W with two GE T700 turboshafts. The US Army's upgraded TOW-armed AH-1F has a laser range-finder and tracker and sophisticated electronics. In 1995, Bell and IAR Brasov signed an agreement covering the licence construction of 96 AH-1Fs in Romania, deliveries commencing in 1999.

Below: **First flown in 1965, the Bell AH-1 serves with the US Army and Marine Corps.** *PRM*

Bell UH-1 Iroquois/412 Griffin

Single-turboshaft medium-lift utility and battlefield helicopter
Basic data for UH-1H
Powerplant: One Avco Lycoming T53-L-13 turboshaft of 1,400eshp (1,045kW)
Rotor diameter: 48ft 0in (14.63m)
Fuselage length: 41ft 10¾in (12.77m)
Max speed: 127mph (204km/h)
Armament: Can be fitted with pintle-mounted machine guns in main cabin doors
Accommodation: Pilot plus up to 14 troops or 3,880lb cargo
First aircraft flown: 1956
Entered service: 1959
Recent/current service: With the US Army, USAF and US Navy and, also in many versions, the air arms of about 50 countries including Argentina, Australia, Austria, Brazil, Canada, Chile, Croatia, Dubai, Germany, Greece, Iran, Italy, Japan, Mexico, Netherlands, New Zealand, Norway, Pakistan, Philippines, Saudi Arabia, Slovenia, South Korea, Spain, Turkey, Uganda and the UK.
Recognition: Large forward cabin with rectangular windows and sliding doors. Engine mounted above the rear of the cabin with the broad-chord two-blade main rotor on a tall pylon. Two-blade tail rotor is on the port side of the tail. Landing skids are located beneath the cabin.
Variants: The UH-1B/UH-1C (Bell 204) had a smaller cabin and low-powered engine; the UH-1D to UH-1L (B205) has the full-size cabin and either the T53-13 or T58-GE-3 turboshaft. Built in Germany by Dornier, in Canada by Canadair and in Italy by Agusta. Various 204s and 205s have been adapted for special duties including ASW, ECM and VIP roles. Larger developments — the UH-1N (Bell 212) with twin PT6 turboshafts and the 214 — have been produced in quantity, followed by the 412 built both by Bell and Agusta. Latest variants are the Bell 412AH/Agusta AB412 Grifone and CH-146 Griffon attack/utility helicopters, while the 412EP flies with the UK services as the Griffin.

Below: **Bell has produced the UH-1 in special military versions for many overseas air arms.**
PRM / DJM

Bell 206 JetRanger/OH-58 Kiowa Warrior

Single-turboshaft utility and observation helicopter
Basic data for OH-58D
Powerplant: One Allison 250-C30R or X turboshaft of 650eshp (484.7kW)
Rotor diameter: 35ft 0in (10.67m)
Fuselage length: 33ft 0in (10.06m)
Max speed: 147mph (236km/h)
Armament: Can be fitted with pintle-mounted machine guns

Accommodation:
Pilot and up to five
passengers
**First aircraft
flown:** December
1962 (Bell 206);
1987 (OH-58D)
Entered service:
May 1968 (B206);
1987
(OH-58D)
Current service:
With the US Army
(OH-58),
US Navy (TH-57),
Canadian Forces
(CH-136), Australia
(CA-36) and

numerous other air arms.

Recognition: Long rectangular cabin with a large
front windscreen and small nose section at its
base. Engine situated above and to the rear of the
cabin with a four-blade main rotor, and tall rotor
mast extending from it, plus a mast-mounted sight
(MMS). Skid undercarriage projects from the
lower edge of the cabin. Thin tailboom has the
rear rotor on the port side and swept fins on the
starboard. A small horizontal surface is at the mid-
boom point.

Variants: The OH-58A Kiowa, TH-57A SeaRanger
and (built by Agusta) AB206A and AB206B are all
similar basic versions. The stretched 206L
LongRanger has been produced as an attack
helicopter with TOW missiles (TexasRanger). The
latest variant is the 406 Combat Scout with

uprated power and transmission and new sight
and weapon systems. Up to 366 OH-58A Kiowas
are being re-manufactured to OH-58D Kiowa
Warrior standard, incorporating Allison 250-C30R
or X turboshafts and new rotors and transmission.
These have two universal weapon pylons and can
carry four Hellfire anti-armour missiles, four
Stinger AAMs, Hydra rocket pods and two half
inch machine guns, in various combinations.

Above and below: The Bell 206 JetRanger/
OH-58 Kiowa utility and observation
helicopter is in service with many air arms.
PRM / APM

Boeing B-52 Stratofortress

Long-range strategic bomber for conventional and ALCM attack

Basic data for B-52H

Powerplant: Eight Pratt & Whitney TF33-P-3 turbofans of 17,000lb st (75.6kN)

Span: 185ft 0in (59.39m)

Length: 160ft 11in (49.05m)

Max speed: 595mph (957km/h)

Armament: Can carry 20 AGM-66B or AGM-129 cruise missiles in the internal bomb bay and on two underwing stations. Conventional munitions include up to eight AGM-84 Harpoon or AGM-142A Have Nap ASMs, AGM-86C cruise missiles, or up to 51 750lb (340kg) iron bombs or mines.

Crew: Five (two pilots, navigator, electronic warfare officer and radar navigator/bombardier)

First aircraft flown: 15 April 1952 (YB-52);

6 March 1961 (B-52H)

Entered service: June 1955 (RB-52B); 9 May 1961 (B-52H)

Current service: With the USAF, in Air Combat Command and AF Reserve Command

Recognition: Long rectangular-section fuselage. Shoulder-mounted wings, angular fin and rudder with almost triangular tailplane. Swept wings

Above and below: **Boeing B-52H Superfortress will remain in service with the USAF into the next century.** *PRM*

have near-constant chord. The eight engines are housed in pairs on pylons which project forward of the wing leading-edge.

Variants: The earlier versions have been retired, the last B-52Gs being phased out in 1994. The B-52H will remain in service for ALCM (Air-Launched Cruise Missile) launching duties into the next century.

Boeing C-135/707

Four-turbojet/turbofan in-flight refuelling tanker/transport, and special mission aircraft

Basic data for KC-135R Stratotanker

Powerplant: Four CFM International F108 turbofans of 22,000lb st (97.9kN)

Span: 130ft 10in (39.88m)

Length: 136ft 3in (41.53m)

Max speed: 609mph (982km/h)

Accommodation: Four crew (and up to 80 passengers in transport guise); up to 120,000lb fuel to transfer in flight.

First aircraft flown: 31 August 1956 (KC-135A); 4 August 1982 (KC-135R)

Entered service: 28 June 1957 (KC-135A); 20 June 1984 (KC-135R)

Current service: Over 600 in service with the USAF, including special missions versions; France, Singapore and Turkey only other KC-135 users. Several air arms have converted Boeing 707/720s in service as transports and tankers.

Recognition: The KC-135 is similar to the Boeing 707/720 but with a windowless fuselage, a large forward freight access door on the port side and a projecting refuelling boom (KC-135 variants) below the tail. Low-set swept narrow-chord wings with underslung engines in four separate pods. Circular narrow body fuselage with the tailplane mounted either side of the tail cone. Tall, narrow fin and rudder, slightly swept.

Variants: More variants of this machine have been designated than any other type of military aircraft. The KC-135 has been the subject of two major re-engining programmes — over 160 AFRs (now AF Reserve Command) and ANG KC-135s were fitted with TF33 turbofans, and titled as KC-135Es. The KC-135R designation applies to those re-engined with F108 (CFM56) turbofans, while KC-135Ts are those examples re-modified after having been configured to refuel the Lockheed

Above: Boeing KC-135R Stratotanker, re-engined with CFM56 engines, here in service with the USAF. *DJM*

SR-71. All the original KC-135As have been retired. The various special mission sub-types are now headed in numbers by the RC-135, adopted for various tasks including the SIGINT and ELINT-gathering roles — however, EC-135 command posts and the pair of OC-135Bs modified for the Open Skies treaty inspection role, and several other versions, remain in service. France flies both KC-135Rs and C-135FR tankers, while operators of further 707 tanker/transport/special mission variants include Argentina, Australia, Brazil (as KC-137s), Chile, Israel, Italy, Saudi Arabia (with its KE-3As), South Africa and Spain.

Boeing E-3 Sentry/AWACS

Four-turbofan airborne warning and control system (AWACS) aircraft
Basic data for E-3D Sentry AEW1
Powerplant: Four CFM International CFM56-2A-3 turbofans of 24,000lb st (106.8kW)
Span: 145ft 9in (44.42m)
Length: 152ft 11in (46.61m)
Max speed: 531mph (855km/h)
Crew: 17
First aircraft flown: 11 February 1972
Entered service: 24 March 1977
Current service: With the USAF, RAF, NATO, France and Saudi Arabia.
Recognition: Similar to the Boeing 707/KC-135 but with the distinctive large circular radar antenna dish set horizontally on two vertical struts extending from the top of the fuselage. Low-set swept narrow-chord wings with underslung engines in four separate pods. Circular narrow-body windowless fuselage with

Above: The Boeing E-3D Sentry equips the RAF's two airborne early warning squadrons, Nos 8 and 23. *PRM*

the tailplane mounted either side of the tail cone. Tall, narrow fin and rudder, slightly swept.
Variants: The USAF's initial E-3A has been developed to the E-3B and E-3C with improved internal equipment, resulting in minor external changes to aerials. The first of seven E-3D Sentry AEW1s for the RAF was delivered in July 1990 and entered service on 1 June 1991. Four similar E-3Fs are now flown by the French Air Force. The RAF's E-3D fleet has wingtip-mounted Loral electronic support measures pods and in-flight refuelling probes, while NATO E-3As are now fitted with ESM with sensors in side-mounted canoe-type fairings.

Boeing E-4/747

Long-range airborne command post and VVIP transport

Basic data for E-4B

Powerplant: Four General Electric F103-GE-100 turbofans of 52,500lb st (233.53kN)

Span: 195ft 8in (59.64m)

Length: 231ft 4in (70.51m)

Max speed: 608mph (978km/h)

Accommodation: Crew of three to eight and up to 50 operators/controllers

First aircraft flown: June 1973 (E-4A)

Entered service: 1974 (E-4A)

Current service: With the USAF as National Emergency Airborne Command Post, Strategic Air Command Control Post and Post-Attack Command & Control Post. Also a VVIP transport with special equipment.

Recognition: Basically a Boeing 747-200. Large fuselage with cockpit set high above the conical-shaped nose. Swept wings set below the fuselage with short engines mounted on pylons projecting forward of the wing. Swept fin, rudder and tailplane with split control surfaces. Multi-bogie main undercarriage which retracts into the lower fuselage. The E-4B has a large fairing on top of the fuselage above the upper-deck compartment.

Variants: Two variants have been built. The initial E-4A had the electronic equipment from the EC-135. The E-4B, which was first flown on 8 June 1978, has specially developed electronics for its specialist roles. It can be recognised by the SHF antenna housing on top of the front fuselage. The VC-25A designation refers to two 747-200s delivered to the USAF to serve as Presidential transports (Air Force One when the President is on board), while a future development will be the YAL-1A airborne laser attack platform testbed — a version of the 747-400. Other military 747 users are Japan and Iran.

Below: **Boeing VC-25A, now used as the US Presidential transport aircraft.** *APM*

Boeing Vertol CH-46 Sea Knight

Twin-turboshaft tandem-rotor medium lift multi-role helicopter
Basic data for CH-46E/KV-107

Powerplant: Two General Electric CT58-GE-16 turboshafts of 1,870eshp (1,395kW)
Rotor diameter: 50ft 0in (15.24m)
Fuselage length: 44ft 10in (13.66m)
Max speed: 165mph (267km/h)
Accommodation: Crew of one to three, plus up to 26 troops or 7,000lb (3,175kg) cargo
First aircraft flown: 16 October 1962
Entered service: June 1964
Current service: With the US Navy and Marine Corps, Canadian Forces, Japanese Defence Forces and Swedish Army, Navy and Air Force.
Recognition: Conventional 'tube' fuselage with circular cabin windows. Front three-blade rotor mounted on a faired pylon above the cockpit; rear rotor above the engines on a taller fairing. Rear loading ramp below the engines. Tricycle undercarriage with nosewheel under the cockpit and main wheels on sponsons projecting from the rear fuselage. Smaller than the CH-47 Chinook.
Variants: The CH-46 (built by Kawasaki as the KV-107) has been progressively developed with improved engine power, avionics and equipment. Swedish HKP-4s are powered by Rolls-Royce Gnome turboshafts; the CH-46E is a more powerful, updated rebuild for the USMC. Canadian CH-113 Labradors will be replaced by EHI Cormorants.

Below: **The Boeing Vertol Sea Knight is a tandem-rotor helicopter used by the US and Swedish Navies.** *PRM*

Boeing CH-47 Chinook

Twin-turboshaft heavy lift tandem-rotor utility helicopter
Basic data for CH-47D
Powerplant: Two AlliedSignal T55-L-714A turboshafts of 4,867eshp (3,629 kW)
Rotor diameter: 60ft 0in (18.29m)
Fuselage length: 51ft 0in (15.54m)
Max speed: 167mph (269km/h)
Armament: The MH-47E version has provision for carriage of 7.62mm Miniguns and a half inch machine gun, plus Stinger AAMs.
Accommodation: Crew of two to four plus up to 44 troops or 26,000lb (11,793kg) payload
First aircraft flown: 21 September 1961 (CH-47A); 11 May 1979 (CH-47D)
Entered service: December 1962 (CH-47A); 28 February 1983 (CH-47D)
Current service: With the US Army, RAF and also air arms in Argentina, Australia, Canada, Egypt, Greece, Iran, Italy, Japan, Libya, Morocco, Netherlands, Singapore, South Korea, Spain, Tanzania, Taiwan and Thailand.
Recognition: Tubular fuselage with fairings along the lower edge to give a flat appearance to the underside. Front rotor blades on a fairing above the cockpit. Engines mounted either side and above the rear fuselage. Rear rotor on a rectangular 'fin' set above the front rotor blade arc. Rear loading ramp. Four-wheel undercarriage with two wheels at the rear and the second pair just beyond halfway along the fuselage.
Variants: There is little external difference in the various models CH-47A to CH-47D, and the examples built by Agusta/Meridionali in Italy and Kawasaki in Japan. The RAF has updated its HC1s to HC2 standard (and bought some new-build aircraft), equivalent to the US Army's CH-47D and thus doubling the payload. Sixteen MH-47E Chinooks are being delivered to the US Army for the Special Operations Force. They feature more powerful engines, in-flight refuelling probe, infra-red linescan and other refinements alongside the armament. The CH-47F is a new, advanced version with different engines, four-blade rotors and an updated cockpit — initial deliveries may be upgrades of existing aircraft.

Below: **Boeing Vertol Chinook HC2, in service with the RAF, is similar to the US Army's CH-47D. PRM**

Boeing (McDonnell Douglas) AH-64 Apache

Twin-turboshaft anti-armour attack helicopter
Basic data for AH-64A
Powerplant: Two General Electric T700-GE-701C turboshafts of 1,890eshp (1,410kW)
Rotor diameter: 48ft 0in (14.63m)
Fuselage length: 49ft 1½in (14.97m)
Max speed: 181mph (293km/h)
Armament: Nose-mounted 30mm M230 Bushmaster chain gun; stub-wing hardpoints for 16 AGM-114 Hellfire missiles or 74 2¾in rockets. Also capability for unguided rockets, Sidewinder, Stinger and Mistral air-to-air and Sidearm anti-radiation missiles.
First aircraft flown: 30 September 1975 (AH-64A); 15 April 1992 (AH-64D)
Entered service: January 1984
Current service: With the US Army and also the air forces of Egypt, Greece, Israel, Netherlands, Saudi Arabia and UAE.
Recognition: Long, narrow fuselage and circular tail boom. Two-place tandem cockpit with TADS/PNVS in the nose. Remote control 30mm gun below the cockpit. Engines either side of the rear fuselage with stub wings below.

Missile/rocket pods carried on pylons below the wings. Fixed main wheel undercarriage with low-pressure tyres. Tail wheel fixed at the extremity of the tail boom. Four-blade tail rotor on the port side of the fin. A conventional tailplane at the base of the rudder.
Variants: AH-64A is the initial production model, used by the US Army and aforementioned overseas operators. The AH-64D has a mast-mounted Lockheed Martin/Westinghouse Longbow millimetre-wave radar. The US Army began modifying its AH-64As to Longbow standard in March 1997 as part of a 10-year programme, with Kuwait and the Royal Netherlands AF both due to receive the new version. Westland-built WAH-64s for the Army Air Corps' order of 67 will also be Longbow-configured, powered by Rolls-Royce/Turboméca RTM332 turboshafts.

Below: **The Boeing (McDonnell Douglas) AH-64A Apache is in service in considerable numbers with the US Army.** *PRM*

Boeing (McDonnell Douglas/Hughes) MD500/530 Defender

Single-turboshaft light attack and utility helicopter

Basic data for MD500MG Defender

Powerplant: One Allison 250-C20B turboshaft of 420eshp (313kW)

Rotor diameter: 26ft 5in (8.05m)

Fuselage length: 23ft 11in (7.29m)

Max speed: 141mph (228km/h)

Armament: Four TOW anti-tank missiles, FN Herstal pods containing 7.62mm or half inch machine guns, or 2¾in rockets in seven- or 12-tube launchers.

First aircraft flown: 27 February 1963 (OH-6A); 4 May 1984 (500MG Defender)

Entered service: 1966

Current service: With the US Army and Argentina, Bahrain, Bolivia, Brazil, Colombia, Costa Rica, Croatia, Cyprus, Denmark, Dominican Republic, El Salvador, Finland, Greece, Indonesia, Israel, Italy, Japan, Jordan, Kenya, Mexico, North Korea, Philippines, South Korea, Spain and Taiwan.

Recognition: Short 'tadpole'-shaped fuselage and tail boom. Glazed front to cabin with landing skids extending from lower side. Engine installed at rear of cabin with jetpipe exhausting below the boom. Five-blade main rotor above the cabin. Weapons carried on small stub wings at the rear. Two-blade tail rotor mounted on port side of tail boom. Dorsal fin with 'T' tailplane and endplates. Ventral fin with a tail skid.

Variants: Original Hughes 500M and US Army OH-6A had lower-powered turboshaft engines and less sophisticated avionics and armament. The

MD500MD Defender is produced in a number of versions as an attack helicopter with a nose- or mast-mounted sight, FLIR and electronic aids, and as an ASW variant with flotation gear, search radar, MAD and naval weapons. Now in production are the MD500MG and 530MG Defenders, the latter with an uprated Allison 250-C30 engine, for anti-armour/attack. In US Army Special Operations Force service are the AH-6G and MH-6 versions (Nightfox 530MGs). Updating the line further, the MD520N and MD600N are equipped with the NOTAR (no tail rotor) system, which may be retrofitted to some earlier examples. The latest development on the theme, the MD900, is also available for military tasks (it is now used by the Belgian Gendarmérie).

Above and below: **A McDonnell Douglas 500 Defender 1 is seen here in Royal Danish AF colours.** *PRM*

British Aerospace Harrier

Single-turbofan single-seat V/STOL day/night ground attack aircraft

Basic data for Harrier GR7

Powerplant: One Rolls-Royce Pegasus Mk 105 vectored-thrust turbofan of 21,500lb st (95.74kN)

Span: 30ft 4in (9.25m)

Length: 47ft 1in (14.35m)

Max speed: 661mph (1,065km/h)

Armament: Two 25mm Royal Ordnance Factories cannon on under-fuselage stations. Nine weapon pylons with 10,800lb (4,900kg) payload. Range of free-fall and retarded bombs, including 1,000lb laser-guided, cluster and practice. Alternatively, or as a mix, rocket launchers, ASMs, Sidewinder/Magic AAMs or other stores. Additional pods can be carried.

First aircraft flown: 18 May 1990

Entered service: 34 new production 1990-2; others conversion of GR5s between 1990-4

Current service: Royal Air Force, with three operational squadrons

Recognition: Large semicircular engine intakes on either side of fuselage forward of wing. A high-set cockpit over the short pointed nose. Broad-chord wing with root extensions and marked anhedral mounted on top of fuselage. The fin is

Above and below: **The British Aerospace Harrier GR7 is the RAF's front line STOVL fighter.** *PRM*

swept on the forward edge with a ventral fillet, with tail cone to rear. The swivelling jet efflux nozzles are situated on the fuselage sides below the wings. The main undercarriage is located under the fuselage with outriggers which retract into wing pods.

Variants: The T4N/T8, a two-seat trainer version of the now retired GR3 is in service with the Royal Navy. The Harrier T10 is the Royal Air Force operational trainer for the GR7, based on the TAV-8B airframe with eight underwing pylons, FLIR and night vision equipment of the GR7.

British Aerospace Hawk

Single-turbofan advanced/operational trainer and light attack/fighter

Basic data for Hawk T1A

Powerplant: One Rolls-Royce/Turboméca Adour turbofan of 5,200lb st (23.16kN)

Span: 30ft 9¾in (9.39m)

Length: 39ft 2in (11.96m)

Max speed: 622mph (1,000km/h)

Armament: One 30mm Aden cannon pack and up to 5,600lb (2,540kg) of underwing stores (rockets, bombs and AIM-9 Sidewinder AAMs).

First aircraft flown: 21 August 1974 (T1)

Entered service: October 1976 (T1)

Current service: With the RAF and RN, and the air arms of Australia (on order), Brunei, Finland, Indonesia, India, Kenya, Kuwait, Oman, Saudi Arabia, South Korea, Switzerland, United Arab Emirates/Dubai Air Wing and Zimbabwe. The US Navy operates T-45A/B/C Goshawks.

Recognition: Slightly-swept wings set at the bottom of the fuselage. Top line of the fuselage curves up from the pointed nose to incorporate the long, clear cockpit canopy then slopes down to the jetpipe, giving a humped appearance. Engine is internally housed with small circular intakes on the lower sides of the fuselage, forward and above the wing roots. Slightly swept vertical and horizontal tail surfaces.

Variants: All RAF Hawks (T1s, T1As and T1Ws)

have inboard pylons for AIM-9 Sidewinder AAMs. Mk 50 and 60 series Hawks for export have uprated Adour Mk 861 engines; some have extra underwing pylons to take 6,800lb (3,085kg) ordnance and improved avionics and attack systems. Finnish AF Hawk Mk 51s were constructed by Valmet, while F&W built the Hawk T66 for the Swiss AF. The USN's T-45 Goshawk is built by McDonnell Douglas, with a modified cockpit and rear fuselage — T-45A for carrier use has twin nosewheel steering, an arrestor hook, twin side air-brakes and a strengthened main undercarriage; T-45B is externally similar, for land use only; T-45C has a digital cockpit. BAe's Hawk 100, an enhanced ground attack derivative, is now in service with several overseas operators. It has been selected for the NATO Flying Training in Canada (NFTC) requirement, to be operated by the Canadian government.

Above and below: **British Aerospace Hawk T1 is the RAF's advanced jet pilot training aircraft, also used by the RN for target duties.** *PRM / APM*

British Aerospace Hawk 200

Single-seat multi-role combat aircraft
Basic data for Hawk 200RDA
Powerplant: One Rolls-Royce/Turboméca Adour Mk871 turbofan of 5,845lb st (26.0kN)
Span: 30ft 9¾in (9.39m); with missiles — 32ft 7in (9.94m)
Length: 37ft 2½in (11.34m)
Max speed: 661mph (1,065km/h)
Armament: None internally. Four underwing pylons capable of 907kg (2,000lb) load, with max 3,493kg (7,700lb) external load. Wingtip rails allow carriage of four Sidewinder or similar AAMs.
First aircraft flown: 19 May 1986
Entered service: 15 August 1994
Current service: With Oman, Indonesia and Malaysia.
Recognition: Slightly swept wings set at the bottom of the fuselage, with fixed wing leading-edge droop to enhance lift and manoeuvrability. Top line of the fuselage curves up from the pointed nose to incorporate a short, domed cockpit canopy. Taller fin than other Hawk variants. Engine is internally housed with small circular intakes on the lower sides of the fuselage and above the wing roots. Slightly swept vertical and horizontal tail surfaces. Enlarged nose to accommodate nose-mounted radar. Chaff/flare dispenser at base of fin. Four underwing pylons and wingtip rails.
Variants: Current versions can perform airspace denial missions, fitted with four Sidewinders, gun and two drop tanks; close air support, with four 1,000lb (454kg) bombs; battlefield interdiction, with 2,000lb (908kg) bomb load; long-range photo-reconnaissance, using a pod containing cameras and infra-red linescan, and Sidewinders for self-defence; and anti-shipping attack fitted with two rocket pods. Mark numbers relate to different purchasing countries.

Below: **British Aerospace Hawk 200, a single-seat multi-role combat version of the Hawk T1.** *PRM*

British Aerospace Sea Harrier

Single-turbofan carrier-based multi-role combat aircraft

Basic data for Sea Harrier FA2

Powerplant: One Rolls-Royce Pegasus 11 Mk 104/106 vectored-thrust turbofan of 21,500lb st (95.74kN)

Span: 25ft 3in (7.70m)

Length: 46ft 5in (14.15m)

Max speed: 736mph (1,185km/h)

Armament: Air-to-air weaponry comprises four AMRAAMs (two mounted underwing and two instead of the underfuselage strakes), or two underwing AMRAAMs plus four Sidewinders. Other options include two BAe Sea Eagle anti-ship, ASRAAM or anti-radar ALARM missiles.

First aircraft flown: 21 August 1978 (FRS1); 19 September 1988 (FRS2, now FA2)

Entered service: September 1979 (FRS1); 2 April 1993 (FRS2, now FA2)

Current service: With the Royal Navy (FA2) and Indian Navy (FRS51)

Recognition: Circular fuselage section with large engine air intakes on either side, forward and below the shoulder-mounted swept wing. The high-set cockpit canopy is set above the engine intakes and slopes down sharply to the pointed nose. The fin is swept on the forward edge. There is a large ventral fillet below the rear fuselage. The main difference from the Harrier GR7 lies in the shape of the nose, raised cockpit and front fuselage.

Variants: The Indian Navy export version of the RN's initial FRS1, the FRS51, remains in service. However, the RN fleet is now entirely made up of the FA2, both converted and new-build aircraft. One major enhancement is the Blue Vixen pulse-Doppler 'track-while-scan' radar.

Top and above: **British Aerospace's Sea Harrier FA2 is the Fleet Air Arm's carrier-borne air defence fighter aircraft.** *PRM / DJM*

CASA C-101 Aviojet

Single-turbofan two-seat jet trainer and ground attack aircraft
Basic data for C-101EB
Powerplant: One AlliedSignal TFE731-2-2J turbofan of 3,500lb st (15.59kN)
Span: 34ft 9½in (10.60m)
Length: 40ft 2in (12.25m)
Max speed: 493mph (793km/h)
Armament: The C-101CC has a 30mm DEFA 533 cannon or twin 12.7mm Browning M3 machine gun pods in its lower fuselage, and six underwing hardpoints for bombs or rocket pods up to a total of 4,960lb (2250kg). C-101DD can carry up to two AGM-65 Maverick ASMs, or two AIM-9 Sidewinders or Matra Magic AAMs.
First aircraft flown: 27 June 1977
Entered service: 17 March 1980
Current service: Operated by the Chilean, Honduran, Jordanian and Spanish air forces.
Recognition: Distinctive cut-away rear fuselage with the whole tail unit projecting behind the jetpipe nozzle. Oval-section fuselage with a tandem cockpit above the tapered nose. Engine intakes either side of the fuselage just forward of the near-constant-chord unswept low-set wings.
Variants: The initial trainer version for the Spanish AF is the C-101EB, while the armed variant with the higher-rated TFE731-3 engine is the C-101BB built in Chile by ENAER. The C-101CC is a light attack version with the more powerful Garrett TFE731-5 of 4,700lb st (20.9kN) which is also fitted to the C-101DD with improved avionics.

Above and below: **A Spanish Air Force CASA C-101 Aviojet advanced trainer.** *PRM / APM*

34

CASA C-212 Aviocar

Twin-turboprop STOL multi-purpose and maritime patrol aircraft
Basic data for C-212-300
Powerplant: Two AlliedSignal TPE 311-10R-513C turboprops of 900eshp (670kW)
Span: 66ft 6in (20.28m)
Length: 53ft 0in (16.15m)
Max speed: 230mph (370km/h)
Armament: Aviocar — two underwing hardpoints of 550lb (250kg) capacity each for carrying twin 7.62mm machine gun pods, a 12.7mm gun pod or 20mm cannon pod. Alternatively, it can be equipped with LAU-3A/32 rocket launchers. Patrullero — torpedoes (Mk 46s or Stingrays), rockets or anti-shipping missiles (Sea Skuas or Aérospatiale AS15TT).
Accommodation: 16 paratroops or 26 passengers; up to 4,410lb (2,000kg) of cargo
First aircraft flown: 26 March 1971
Entered service: 1973 (Series 200); 1984 (Series 300)
Current service: With the armed forces of Abu Dhabi, Angola, Bolivia, Chad, Chile, Colombia, Djibouti, Equatorial Guinea, France, Indonesia, Jordan, Lesotho, Myanmar, Nicaragua, Panama, Portugal, South Africa, Spain, Sudan, Sweden, Thailand, Uruguay, Venezuela and Zimbabwe.
Recognition: Twin turboprops mounted forward of the high, straight wing. A rectangular fuselage, with a short, pointed nose and upswept rear section. An angular fin and rudder with a large dorsal extension. Undercarriage fairings on the lower fuselage below the wing. Tailplane positioned below the fin and rudder on an extension of the fuselage. Series 300 has a redesigned nose, extended wingtips and can carry two 500-litre auxiliary fuel tanks on underwing stations.
Variants: The main military version is the C-212A utility transport, with the latest Series 300 featuring winglets. Designated C-212MP Patrullero, the maritime patrol derivative has a search radar in the nose radome. Other service variants include those modified for ECM, photographic and SAR roles.

Below: **CASA C-212 Aviocar light transport is operated by the Spanish Air Force.** *PRM*

Dassault Atlantic/Atlantique 2

Twin-turboprop long-range maritime patrol and anti-submarine aircraft
Basic data for Atlantique 2
Powerplant: Two Rolls-Royce/SNECMA Tyne 21 turboprops of 6,100eshp (4,550kW)
Span: 122ft 10in (37.45m)
Length: 123ft 9in (37.71m)
Max speed: 403mph (648km/h)
Armament: All types of NATO bombs, torpedoes, depth charges, mines and missiles may be carried in the bomb-bay. Four underwing pylons may carry 7,716lb (3,500kg) of stores, including ASMs and AAMs.
Crew: 10
First aircraft flown: 21 October 1961 (BR1150); May 1981 (Atlantique 2)
Entered service: 10 December 1965 (BR1150); 1989 (Atlantique 2)
Current service: With the navies of France, Germany, Italy and Pakistan.
Recognition: Long double-bubble fuselage with a short rounded nose which has wrap-around cockpit windows. A large fin with dorsal extension; the tapered-chord tailplane has a pronounced dihedral. A large boom extends beyond the fin and tailplane. Straight upswept wings are set in mid-fuselage with engines mounted in nacelles forward of the wing. The Atlantique 2 features a Tango FLIR sensor in a chin turret.
Variants: The original BR1150 Atlantic has now been superseded by the Atlantique 2 which features an improved air-to-air and air-to-surface-ship capability, and updated electronics. This version is only in French Navy service, though German and Italian BR1150s have recently undergone upgrade programmes, including fitment of new radar, sonar and ESM equipment. Five German aircraft are equipped for ELINT tasks.

Below: **The Dassault Atlantic/Atlantique 2 serves as a long-range anti-submarine aircraft.** *PRM*

Dassault Falcon 20/Gardian

Twin-turbofan maritime patrol aircraft/VIP transport

Basic data for Falcon 20C

Powerplant: Two Garrett ATF3 turbofans of 4,250lb st (18.92kN)

Span: 53ft 5¾in (16.30m)

Length: 56ft 3in (17.14m)

Max speed: 540mph (869km/h)

Accommodation: Two crew and up to 14 passengers

First aircraft flown:
1 January 1965

Entered service: 1979

Current service: With the US Coast Guard (HU-25A/B Guardian), French Navy (Falcon 20H Gardian) and Chilean Navy, while Falcon 20s are contracted from FR Aviation in the UK for target-towing, fighter direction and ECM training by RN and RAF. Used as a transport by the air forces of France, Norway (which also flies Falcon 20ECMs), Portugal, Spain and others worldwide.

Recognition: Circular fuselage with a broad swept fin and rudder, having the tailplane mounted midway up. The engines are carried in pods on either side of the fuselage forward of the tail. The low-set wings are swept and some aircraft have underwing hardpoints for target towing and electronic pods.

Variants: The VIP transport was developed from the executive jet. There is little external change in the HU-25A Guardian which is equipped with Varan pulse-compression search radar, Omega and INAS; similarly the Falcon 20H Gardian of the French Navy, used in the Pacific, has an extensive avionics package. Various Falcon 20s of the French AF have been fitted with Mirage radars for crew training.

Below: **Dassault Falcon 20s are widely used as a maritime patrol and ECM aircraft.** *PRM*

Dassault Mirage F1

Single-turbojet single-seat fighter/attack aircraft

Basic data for Mirage F1C

Powerplant: One SNECMA Atar 9K-50 turbojet of 11,025lb st (49.0kN) dry and 15,785lb st (70.2kN) with afterburner

Span: 27ft 7in (8.40m)

Length: 50ft 2½in (15.30m)

Max speed: 1,449mph (2,338km/h)

Armament: Two 30mm DEFA 553 cannon, AIM-9 Sidewinder or Matra Magic AAMs on wingtips plus up to 8,820lb (4,000kg) of external stores on five pylons.

First aircraft flown: 23 December 1966

Entered service: 14 March 1973

Current service: With the air arms of Ecuador, France, Greece, Iraq, Jordan, Kuwait, Libya, Morocco, Qatar, South Africa and Spain.

Recognition: Long sleek fuselage, pointed nose and shoulder-mounted swept wings. Streamlined cockpit canopy forward of the semicircular engine intakes on either side of the fuselage. Swept fin and rudder with a rounded top; two ventral strakes below the swept tailplane.

Variants: The F1A is a basic attack aircraft which has been improved and refined into the multi-role F1E for export; the F1C is the interceptor version and the F1CR a reconnaissance fighter with infra-red sensors and cameras. The F1B and F1D are two-seat trainers. Export variants are given different suffixes to denote the country. A total of 55 French AF F1Cs have been converted to F1CT tactical combat aircraft and fitted with an updated version of the F1CR's nav/attack system.

Below and bottom: **The Mirage F1 is used as an attack/interceptor aircraft.** *PRM / DJM*

Dassault Mirage 2000

Single-turbofan, single-seat long-range air superiority fighter
Basic data for Mirage 2000C
Powerplant: One SNECMA M53-5 turbofan of 12,235lb st (54.43kN) dry and 19,840lb st (88.26kN) with afterburner
Span: 29ft 11in (9.13m)
Length: 47ft 1½in (14.36m)
Max speed: 1,518mph (2,440km/h)
Armament: Two 30mm DEFA 554 cannon plus two Matra Super 530S and two Matra R550 Magic air-to-air missiles plus five under-fuselage hardpoints, with a maximum load of 13,890lb (6,300kg). ASMs that can be carried include 250kg bombs (up to 18), 400kg modular stand-off/area bombs (up to six), runway denial and cluster bombs, and Armat anti-radiation or Exocet anti-ship missiles. French AF 2000Ds and Ns can carry the Aérospatiale ASMP stand-off nuclear missile, and Ds the Matra Apache stand-off weapon containing sub-munitions.
First aircraft flown: 10 March 1978
Entered service: February 1983
Current service: With the air forces of Egypt, France, Greece, India, Peru, Qatar, Taiwan and UAE.

Recognition: Large delta wing extending from the engine intakes to the rear of the aircraft. Swept angular fin with the jetpipe extending beyond the rudder trailing-edge. A pointed nose with semicircular intakes mounted either side of the fuselage.
Variants: The highly capable and agile Mirage 2000 has been produced in four main variants, namely the 2000B — two-seat conversion/operational trainer; 2000C — single-seat air superiority fighter; 2000N — two-seat low altitude strike (a mixture of N-K1s, nuclear-only aircraft, and N-K2s with an additional conventional capability); and the 2000R — the single-seat reconnaissance version. Now in French AF service is the 2000D, a development of the N but with only conventional weapons capability. The Mirage 2000E is the single-seat multi-role export version, while the 2000-5 is the latest advanced multi-role combat version. Other designations refer to the purchasing country, such as the 2000EG for Greece, 2000H for India and Peru's 2000P.

Above: **Dassault Mirage 2000B operated by the French Air Force.** *PRM*

Dassault Rafale

Twin-turbofan, single-seat advanced fighter

Basic data for Rafale C

Powerplant: Two SNECMA M88-2 augmented turbofans of 10,950lb st (48.7kN) dry and 16,400lb st (72.9kN) with afterburner

Span: 35ft 9¼in (10.90m) over wingtip missiles

Length: 50ft 2¼in (15.30m)

Max speed: 1,317mph (2,125km/h)

Armament: One internal 30mm Giat DEFA 791B cannon, plus up to 13,230lb (6,000kg) of ordnance carried on 14 external hardpoints (six underwing, two wingtip, two centreline and four underwing stations). Weapons include an ASMP stand-off nuclear bomb, up to eight Matra Mica AAMs (with IR or active homing), LGBs, AM39 Exocet anti-ship missiles, AS30L laser-guided ASMs, or Apache dispensers with anti-armour or anti-runway munitions.

First aircraft flown: 4 July 1986 (Rafale A demonstrator); 19 May 1991 (Rafale C)

Entered service: To enter service from 1999

Recognition: Delta configuration with small swept canards forward of leading-edge of delta. Engine intakes are positioned in the lower fuselage sides behind the cockpit. Large swept fin and rudder. Sharply pointed nose with large glazed cockpit cover. Wingtip-mounted missiles.

Variants: The French AF production versions are the single-seat Rafale C and two-seat Rafale B, the latter intended as the primary combat version with some 140 expected to be built. They will replace Jaguars and Mirage F1s. The carrier-capable Rafale M for the French Navy is to supersede the F-8P Crusader.

Above and below: **The single-seat Rafale C is expected to be in service with the French Air Force in 1999.** *PRM / APM*

Dassault Super Etendard

Single-seat carrier-borne strike fighter
Basic data for Super Etendard
Powerplant: One SNECMA Atar 8K-50 turbojet of 11,023lb st (49.0kN)
Span: 31ft 5¾in (9.60m)
Length: 46ft 11½in (14.31m)
Max speed: 746mph (1,200km/h)
Armament: Two 30mm DEFA cannon and up to 4,630lb (2,100kg) of external stores on centreline and wing pylons. Weapons include rocket pods, bombs (including LGBs), Magic AAMs, two AM39 Exocet anti-ship missiles or one ASMP guided stand-off nuclear missile.

First aircraft flown:
28 October 1974
Entered service: June 1978
Current service: With the navies of France and Argentina.
Recognition: Swept wings mounted low/mid on fuselage aft of twin engine intakes. Large broad swept fin with a swept tailplane mounted just above the fuselage. The cockpit is well forward on a tapered nose section.
Variants: The upgrade of the French Navy's fleet of Super Etendards with new radar and avionics has given the aircraft a life extension until 2008.

Below and right:
Dassault-Breguet Super Etendard, the French Navy's carrier-borne fighter. *PRM*

41

Dassault/Dornier Alpha Jet

Twin-turbofan two-seat trainer/light strike aircraft

Basic data for Alpha Jet E

Powerplant: Two SNECMA-Turboméca Larzac 04-C6 turbofans of 2,976lb st (13.24kN)

Span: 29ft 11in (9.11m)

Length: 38ft 6½in (11.75m)

Max speed: 621mph (1,000km/h)

Armament: Removable underfuselage container for a 30mm DEFA or 27mm Mauser cannon pod, bombs and rockets on five pylons. On updated versions, Magic AAMs can be carried for self-defence, and Maverick ASMs for the attack role.

First aircraft flown: 26 October 1973

Entered service: 4 November 1978

Current service: In addition to the French AF (Germany having retired its fleet of Alpha Jet As), it is also in service in Belgium, Cameroon, Egypt, Ivory Coast, Morocco, Nigeria, Portugal, Qatar and Togo.

Recognition: Slim fuselage with a long cockpit canopy. Short-span swept wings which are set high on the fuselage, above the rounded side intakes for the internally-mounted engines. The rear fuselage extends above the twin jetpipes with a swept fin and tailplane at the extremity.

Variants: Versions produced are the Alpha Jet E — trainer/light attack; Alpha Jet A — close attack; Alpha Jet 2 — improved close support, with uprated Larzac 04-C20 engines; and finally the Alpha Jet ATS (Advanced Training System, previously known as Alpha Jet 3), developed by Dassault to match the evolution of cockpit systems in future combat aircraft. The standard aircraft has been licence-built in Egypt.

Below: The Dassault-Breguet/Dornier Alpha Jet here operated as an advanced trainer with the Portuguese Air Force. *PRM*

De Havilland (Bombardier) DHC-8 Dash 8

Twin-engined multi-mission STOL utility aircraft

Basic data for Dash 8M Series 100

Powerplant: Two Pratt & Whitney Canada PW120A turboprops of 2,000eshp (1,490kW)

Span: 85ft 0in (25.91m)

Length: 73ft 0in (22.25m)

Max speed: 311mph (500km/h)

Accommodation: 36 passengers in commuter trim or up to 9,849lb (4,467kg) as a freighter. Can also be flown in 'combi' configuration.

First aircraft flown: 20 June 1983

Entered service: September 1988

Current service: With the Canadian Forces, Kenya and the USAF.

Recognition: Narrow profile turbo-props set underneath high-set, narrow-chord, unswept wings. Circular fuselage section which sweeps up to a broad, slightly swept, rectangular fin and rudder. Dorsal extension reaches forward to the trailing-edge of the wing. Straight tailplane set on top of the fin. Streamlined nose with a continuous line down from the cockpit.

Variants: Canadian Forces CC-142 transports have long-range fuel tanks, rough-field landing gear, strengthened floors while the CT-142 is a navigation trainer with an extended nose for its radar. US Air Force E-9As, used for range support, are equipped with ventral AN/APS-128D sea surveillance radar and a steerable phased-array telemetry antenna in a box fairing on the starboard side of the fuselage

Below: **Dash 8s are operated by several air arms for transport and navigational training.** *PRM*

EH Industries Merlin

Three-engined multi-role helicopter, with naval, utility, SAR and civil variants
Basic data for Merlin HM1/HC3

Powerplant: Three Rolls-Royce/Turboméca RTM322 turboshafts of 2,312eshp (1,723kW) for Royal Navy and RAF versions; General Electric T700-GE-T6A turboshafts of 1,714shp (1,278kW) in Italian naval variant.

Rotor diameter: 61ft 0in (18.59m)

Fuselage length: 64ft 0in (19.51m)

Max speed: 192mph (309km/h)

Armament: Naval version able to carry up to four Marconi Stingray homing torpedoes, or anti-shipping missiles. Utility version can be fitted with stub wings for rocket pods and a 12.7mm machine gun in a chin turret. Machine guns can be pintle-mounted at cabin doors.

Accommodation: Utility version can accommodate 30 equipped troops or 16 stretchers. Maximum external underslung load of 12,000lb (5,445kg).

First aircraft flown: 9 October 1987

Enters service: 1999 delivery for RN and 2000 for RAF

Recognition: Long fuselage with a flat boat-hull bottom and large sponsons into which the main undercarriage wheels retract. Three engines mounted above the cabin with the five-blade rotor on top. Blades feature a paddle at the tips. Four-blade tail rotor on top of the port side of the fin and pronounced tailplane at base of fin. The naval version has a nose-mounted radar and folding tail. The utility version has a rear loading ramp.

Variants: Joint venture between Agusta and GKN Westland; civil variants are the EH101-500 Utility with rear ramp and EH101-300 Heliliner passenger versions, both with CTT-6 engines; the naval Merlin HM1 includes ASW, ASV and SAR derivatives, and the military utility Merlin HC3 for the RAF will perform tactical troop lift, logistic support, combat search and rescue, casualty evacuation and command and control. The Canadian Armed Forces has ordered 15 SAR versions of the utility helicopter, named Cormorant.

Below: **Westland/Agusta's EHI Merlin HM1 is due to enter service with the Royal Navy in 1999.** *PRM*

ENAER T-35 Pillán

Single piston-engined tandem two-seat primary/basic trainer
Basic data for T-35 Pillán
Powerplant: One Textron Lycoming AEIO-540-K1K5 piston engine of 300hp (225kW)
Span: 29ft 0in (8.84m)
Length: 26ft 3in (8.00m)
Max speed: 193mph (311km/h)
First aircraft flown: 6 March 1981 (T-35); March 1991 (T-35DT)
Entered service: 31 July 1985
Current service: With the air forces of Chile, Panama, Paraguay and Spain.
Recognition: Low-set unswept wings without tip tanks, fuselage fillet at base of leading-edge of wing. Large clearview canopy covering the tandem cockpit. Tailplane low set at rear base of fin and rudder. Fin is slightly swept.

Variants: The ENAER Pillán is based on Piper's PA-28 Dakota and PA-32 Saratoga. T-35A is a primary trainer and T-35B an instrument trainer for the Chilean Air Force, while the T-35C was built for the Spanish AF as the E26 Tamiz, and the T-35D for the Panamanian AF as an instrument trainer. The T-35DT Turbo Pillán is a re-engined version, itself a development of ENAER's own T-35TX Aucan, and powered by an Allison 250-B17D of 420shp (313kW) — converted by the Soloy Corporation in the USA, it is yet to receive any orders.

Below: **The ENAER T-35 Pillán two-seat basic trainer is produced in Chile.** *PRM*

Eurocopter (Aérospatiale) AS332 Super Puma/ AS532 Cougar

Twin-turboshaft multi-role helicopter
Basic data for AS532U-2 Cougar
Powerplant: Two Turboméca Makila 1A2 turboshafts of 1,657eshp (1,236kW)
Rotor diameter: 53ft 2in (16.2m)

Fuselage length: 54ft 11in (16.74m)
Max speed: 170mph (273km/h)
Armament: Guns and rocket pods may be fitted to army-configured aircraft, while naval versions can carry two AM39 Exocet anti-ship missiles or homing torpedoes.

Accommodation: Up to 28 passengers or 20 fully-equipped troops
First aircraft flown: 13 September 1978 (AS332)
Entered service: 1981 (AS332)
Current service: With many air arms including those of Argentina, Brazil, Chile, China, Democratic Republic of Congo, France, Germany, Indonesia, Japan, Jordan, Kuwait, Malaysia, Netherlands, Qatar, Saudi Arabia, Singapore, Spain, Sweden, Switzerland, Turkey, UAE and Venezuela.
Recognition: Largely similar to the standard Puma, but with a more pointed nose and larger sponsons on the fuselage sides (sometimes containing flotation gear). The cabin windows are more numerous and also larger. A tail bumper with skid is prominent.
Variants: The original military version was the AS332B Super Puma, followed by the AS332M which has a stretched fuselage, some 76cm (30in) longer and allowing an increased payload. The corresponding civil derivatives were the AS332C and AS332L. From 1990, the designation was changed to AS532 Cougar, a number of additional sub-types being developed, the latest being the AS532U-2 which has seen another fuselage stretch. The French Army's HORIZON battlefield surveillance radar is fitted to modified AS532ULs, while the standard Cougar continues to replace the service's SA330 Pumas. The naval AS532SC, as flown by Saudi Arabia, can be Exocet-equipped.

Above and below: Aérospatiale's AS332 Super Puma entered service in 1981 and serves with 22 air arms. *APM / PRM*

Eurocopter (Aérospatiale) AS350 Ecureuil/AS550 Fennec

Single-turboshaft six-seat general purpose helicopter

Basic data for AS550A-2 Fennec
Powerplant: One Turboméca Arriel 1D1 turboshaft of 858eshp (640kW)
Rotor diameter: 35ft ¾in (10.69m)
Fuselage length: 35ft 10½in (10.93m)
Max speed: 178mph (287km/h)
Armament: TOW or Mistral missiles, 7.62mm machine guns, a 20mm GIAT gun pod, and rocket pods; up to two torpedoes on naval versions.
Accommodation: Six seats
First aircraft flown: 21 June 1974 (AS350); 27 September 1979 (AS355)
Entered service: 1976
Current service: In service or ordered for the air arms of Abu Dhabi, Argentina, Australia, Benin, Botswana, Brazil, Central African Republic, Comores, Denmark, Djibouti, Eire, France, Malawi, Paraguay, Peru, Sierra Leone and Singapore, plus the UK armed services.

Recognition: Tadpole-shaped fuselage with glazed front and side cabin windows and two oval nose windows. The three-blade main rotor is mounted above the powerplant aft of the cabin. Fixed skids extend from the fuselage. A conventional tail rotor is on the starboard side.

Variants: Original AS350 is a six-seat utility helicopter. The AS355 Ecureuil 2 (now AS555 Fennec) has two Allison 250-C20F turboshafts, wider-chord main rotor blades, strengthened airframe and landing skids — it can be equipped with missiles, gun/rocket packs or M621 cannon. The AS550A-2 Fennec is the military battlefield version, the M-2 being the naval variant; AS555AN is the twin-engined battlefield derivative.

Below: **A military derivative of the AS350 Ecureuil is this AS550 Fennec.** *DJM*

Eurocopter (Aérospatiale) AS365 Dauphin II/ AS565 Panther

Twin-turboshaft multi-role helicopter
Basic data for AS565AA Panther
Powerplant: Two Turboméca Arriel 1M1 turboshafts of 783eshp (585kW)
Rotor diameter: 39ft 1in (11.93m)
Fuselage length: 38ft 2in (11.63m)
Max speed: 178mph (287km/h)
Armament: Mistral air-to-air and eight HOT anti-tank missiles, two 20mm cannon and rocket pods
Accommodation: Crew of two and up to nine passengers/eight troops
First aircraft flown: 29 February 1984 (AS365M)
Entered service: 1984
Current service: With the air arms of Angola, Brazil, Cameroon, Chile, China, Eire, France, India, Ivory Coast, Malawi, Saudi Arabia and the US Coast Guard.
Recognition: Four-blade single main rotor above the twin turboshafts which are above and to the rear of the cabin. A tapered rear fuselage with a fenestron tail rotor built into the vertical tail surface. The small tailplane is set either side of the rear fuselage and has endplates. The stepped nose includes a radar antenna. Armament is carried on outriggers alongside the cabin.
Variants: AS365F (formerly SA365F) is a naval helicopter for search and rescue duties and air-to-surface attack; an ASW variant is the latest development. SA366 was produced for the US Coast Guard as the HH-65A Dolphin, SA365K is a more powerful twin-Arriel variant. The AS565 Panther (previously SA365M) is the current production version — an army attack type with more powerful Turboméca TM333 turboshafts, sliding cabin doors, HOT missiles and two 20mm cannon or other military equipment. It is now in French Navy service. Harbin in China also builds the AS365N transport.

Below: **Entering service in 1984 the AS365 Dauphin II has been exported to eight military customers.** *PRM*

Eurocopter (MBB) BO105

Twin-turboshaft light utility and attack helicopter

Basic data for BO105CB

Powerplant: Two Allison 250-C20B turboshafts of 420eshp (320kW)

Rotor diameter: 32ft 3in (9.84m)

Length: 28ft 1in (8.56m)

Max speed: 167mph (270km/h)

Armament: Can carry six Euromissile HOT anti-tank missiles in two three-tube launchers, mounted on fuselage outriggers. Swedish versions may operate with ESCO HeliTOW anti-tank missiles.

First aircraft flown: 16 February 1967

Entered service: 1969

Current service: With the German Army (BO105M for observation and communications, BO105P for anti-armour duties), Bahrain, Chile, Colombia, Indonesia, Kenya, Mexico, Netherlands, Peru, Philippines, Sierra Leone, Spain, Sudan, Sweden and UAE.

Recognition: Short deep fuselage with a full-glazed nose section. Engine behind the cabin with the four-blade rigid main rotor above. Short boom carrying the tail rotor on the port side. Tailplane with endplates either side of the boom. Landing skids extend from the lower edge of the cabin.

Variants: Three main versions have been built — the BO105CB is the standard utility transport; the BO105M has been developed for the German Army for air observation and liaison, and the BO105P for anti-tank and anti-armour duties. The BO105CBS is for SAR operations, and the BO105LS is a hot-and-high version (built in Canada) with C250-C28C engines.

Above and right:
MBB BO105P is the standard communications, observation and anti-tank helicopter with numerous air arms.
PRM

Eurocopter Tiger/Tigre

Twin-engined anti-tank and combat support helicopter
Basic data for Tiger HAP
Powerplant: Two MTU/Rolls-Royce/Turboméca MTR390 turboshafts of 1,285eshp (958kW)
Rotor diameter: 42ft 7⅞in (13.00m)
Fuselage length: 45ft 11in (14.00m)
Max speed: 200mph (322km/h)
Armament: One 30mm GIAT AM-30781 automatic cannon in undernose turret; four Matra Mistral air-to-air missiles and two pods each with 22 x 68mm unguided SNEB rockets on underwing pylons.
First aircraft flown: 27 April 1991
Entered service: For delivery to the French Army in 1999
Recognition: Long, narrow slab-sided fuselage. Two stepped cockpits (with pilot in front) with large flat-plate transparencies. Remote-control gun below the cockpit. Engines are mounted side-by-side above the centre fuselage, over small stub wings with anhedral. Non-retractable tailwheel-type landing gear, with single wheel on each unit. Four-blade main rotor. Horizontal tail towards the rear of the boom, with endplate fins. Long infra-red suppressors fitted to engine exhausts, which are diverted upwards. Three-blade tail rotor mounted high on starboard side of fin. Mast-mounted sight may be fitted.
Variants: The Tiger is currently being developed in three versions, differing in equipment and weapons fit. The HAP is the French Army's escort/fire support version; the HAC is the French anti-tank version. The German Army's UHU is a multi-role anti-tank/support helicopter.

Below: **Due to enter service with the French Army in 1999 is the Eurocopter Tiger twin-engined anti-tank helicopter.** *PRM*

Eurofighter

Single-seat, highly agile STOL-capable fighter, optimised for air defence/air superiority; secondary capability for ground attack

Basic data for Eurofighter

Powerplant: Two Eurojet EJ200 advanced technology afterburning turbofans of 13,490lb st (60.08kN)

Span: 34ft 5½in (10.50m)

Length: 47ft 7in (14.50m)

Max speed: 1,321mph (2,125km/h)

Armament: Interceptor has internally mounted 27mm Mauser gun in starboard wing root, plus mix of medium-range AIM-120 AMRAAM or Aspide and short-range air-to-air missiles carried externally. Total of 13 external stores stations; five (including one wet) under fuselage and four (including one wet) under each wing. Maximum load 14,300lb (6,500kg). Attack stores include 1,000lb bombs, BL755, laser-guided bombs and ALARM missiles.

First aircraft flown: 27 March 1994 (DA1 — Germany); 6 April 1994 (DA2 — UK)

Entered service: Planned to enter service in 2001

Recognition: Low-wing, low aspect ratio tailless delta with 53° leading-edge sweepback. Underfuselage box with side-by-side engine air intakes. Engines mounted side-by-side in rear fuselage. All moving canard foreplanes below windscreen. Airbrake aft of canopy, forming part of dorsal spine. Nose radome and fin-tip GFRP. Tall swept fin and rudder. Single-wheel main landing gear units retract inward into fuselage, nosewheel forward. Retractable probe for in-flight refuelling. Rear-hinged clamshell canopy.

Variants: The only main derivative to date is the two-seater, with full avionics and armament as a combat-capable conversion trainer. It was reported in 1998 that the Eurofighter is to be named Typhoon in service.

Above: Eurofighter is expected to enter service with the RAF, German, Italian and Spanish Air Forces.

Fairchild Republic A-10 Thunderbolt II

Twin-turbofan close support/strike aircraft

Basic data for A-10A/OA-10A

Powerplant: Two General Electric TF34-GE100 turbofans of 9,065lb st (40.3kN)

Span: 57ft 6in (17.53m)

Length: 53ft 4in (16.25m)

Max speed: 517mph (835km/h)

Armament: One 30mm multi-barrel GAU-8 Avenger rotary cannon in the nose and up to 16,000lb (7,257kg) of ordnance under the wings and fuselage. Eleven underwing and underfuselage hardpoints can carry AGM-65 Maverick anti-armour missiles, bombs (cluster, laser-guided and conventional), and AIM-9 Sidewinders.

First aircraft flown: 5 April 1972

Entered service: Spring 1976

Current service: Only with the USAF.

Recognition: Long pencil-shaped fuselage with large engine pods attached either side of it, just forward and above the level of the tailplane. Twin large fins mounted at each end of the rectangular tailplane. The straight narrow-chord wings are set at the bottom of the fuselage. Fairings under the wing partly accommodate the stalky main undercarriage legs and wheels. A protruding cockpit canopy rises above the short, rounded nose.

Variants: A number of A-10As have been redesignated as OA-10As, operating in the forward air control role without any modification to the aircraft.

Below: **USAF's distinctive anti-tank aircraft, the Fairchild Republic A-10A Thunderbolt II. PRM**

FMA IA63 Pampa

Single turbofan two-seat basic/advanced trainer

Basic data for IA63 Pampa

Powerplant: One Garrett TFE371-2-2N turbofan of 3,500lb st (15.57kN)

Span: 31ft 9½in (9.67m)

Length: 35ft 9¼in (10.90m)

Max speed: 465mph (750km/h)

Armament: One 30mm cannon pod on fuselage centreline. Ordnance load of 3,415lb (1,550kg) distributed between centreline and four underwing stations.

First aircraft flown: 6 October l984

Entered service: 15 March l988

Current service: 64 were initially ordered and are now operational with the Argentine AF, with 12 likely for the Argentine Navy.

Recognition: Straight leading-edge wings set at shoulder level on fuselage. Top line of the fuselage curves up from the pointed nose to incorporate the long clear cockpit canopy. Distinctive cut-away rear fuselage with the whole tail unit projecting behind the jetpipe nozzle. Engine intakes either side of the fuselage. Anhedral tailplane.

Variants: Developed by Dornier for the Argentine Government and built by FMA. A continuing update programme for the Pampa is based around the integration of the Elbit lightweight weapon delivery and navigation system.

Below: **FMA IA63 Pampa two-seat basic/advanced trainers are in service with the Argentine Air Force.** *PRM*

Fokker F-27/50/60 Utility

Twin-turboprop medium-range tactical transport and maritime patrol aircraft
Basic data for Fokker 50
Powerplant: Two Pratt & Whitney Canada PW125B turboprops of 2,500eshp (1,864kW)
Span: 95ft 2in (29.00m)
Length: 82ft 10in (25.25m)
Max speed: 261mph (420km/h)
Armament: The Maritime Enforcer 2 has two fuselage and six underwing hardpoints for a range of weapons including mines, torpedoes, depth charges and a range of anti-ship missiles (Harpoon, Exocet, Sea Eagle or Sea Skua).
Accommodation: Three crew plus 50 paratroops or 30 stretchers
First aircraft flown: 24 November 1955 (F-27); 28 December 1985 (Fokker 50); 2 November 1995 (60 Utility)
Entered service: November 1958 (F-27); May 1996 (60 Utility)
Current service: With the governments and air arms of Algeria, Argentina, Bolivia, Finland, Ghana, Guatemala, India, Indonesia, Iran, Ivory Coast, Myanmar, Netherlands, Pakistan, Peru, Philippines, Senegambia, Singapore, Spain, Sudan, Thailand and Uruguay.
Recognition: Long oval-section fuselage with narrow-chord high-mounted straight wings. The engines, with six-blade propellers, are carried beneath the wings in nacelles extending fore and aft of the wing. The fin has a dorsal extension along the length of the rear fuselage, with the tailplane at the fin base. The nose contour is broken by the wrap-around cockpit windows.
Variants: The original military F-27-300M has now been retired from Royal Netherlands AF service, but variants of the basic F-27 remain in use as transports in several countries — these include the F-27-400M, with more powerful engines, and the stretched Mk 500; optimised for such roles as SAR, maritime patrol and coastguard duties, the F-27 Maritime (in various marks) is a further derivative. The Fokker 50, an updated development, is also offered in various military guises — apart from the basic passenger/VIP transport, there are the Maritime 2 and Enforcer 2, and now the Fokker 60 Utility. This stretched version, with an 88ft 2in (26.87m) fuselage, is in Royal Netherlands AF service equipped with a large cargo door and offers significant performance and payload advantages over its F-27 predecessor.

Below: **In May 1996, the first Fokker 60 Utility was delivered to the Royal Netherlands Air Force.** *DJM*

GKN Westland Lynx

Light utility and shipborne ASW/SAR helicopter

Basic data for Lynx HMA8

Powerplant: Two Rolls-Royce Gem 42-1 turboshafts of 1,135eshp (845kW)

Rotor diameter: 42ft 0in (12.80m)

Length: 39ft 1½in (11.92m)

Max speed: 207mph (333km/h)

Armament: Four Sea Skua anti-ship missiles, two Mk 44/46 or Stingray torpedoes or Mk II depth charges in ASW configuration; Army variants can be equipped with eight TOW anti-tank missiles and other battlefield weapons.

Accommodation: Crew of two/three plus up to 10 passengers

First aircraft flown: 21 March 1971 (WG13 prototype)

Entered service: September 1976 (HAS2); May 1992 (HAS8, now HMA8)

Current service: With the RN, Army Air Corps and RM, and the French Navy; also in service in Brazil, Denmark, Germany, Netherlands, Nigeria, Norway, Portugal and South Korea.

Recognition: Short cabin with a stepped-up tail boom, cockpit set above a conical nose with radar in most ASW versions. Engines mounted above the cabin, with a four-blade main rotor. Large sliding cabin doors with a single square window. Tricycle undercarriage (Naval variants) or skids (utility/Army versions). Four-blade rotor on port side of tail with small tailplane on starboard.

Variants: There are two basic versions — the Army derivatives, with the AH7 (a more powerful conversion of the earlier AH1) and wheeled AH9 in service with the AAC; and naval Lynxes, the RN using HAS3s and the new HMA8 (equipped with new rotor blades and Sea Spray radar), and the French Navy HAS2(FN)s and HAS4(FN)s. The export Super Lynx, recently sold to Brazil (Mk 21A), Portugal (Mk 95) and South Korea (Mk 99), is similar to the HMA8 with various mark numbers denoting operators. Equally, earlier naval Lynx versions for different nations have been given their own designations — for instance, the Royal Danish Navy's Mk 80 and 90, and the Mk 88 of the German Navy. All the Royal Netherlands Navy's examples have been upgraded to SH-14D standard with more powerful engines and improved systems.

Above: **GKN Westland Lynxes have been delivered in army and naval versions.** *PRM*

Grumman EA-6 Prowler

Twin-turbojet four-seat carrier-based electronic warfare aircraft

Basic data for EA-6B

Powerplant: Two Pratt & Whitney J52-P-408 turbojets of 11,200lb st (49.82kN)

Span: 53ft 0in (16.15m)

Length: 59ft 10in (18.24m)

Max speed: 383mph (617km/h)

Armament: Normally unarmed but can carry a wide range of stores of up to 14,000lb, including HARM anti-radiation missiles on four wing pylons.

Crew: Four (pilot and three ECM officers)

First aircraft flown: 25 May 1968

Entered service: 2 May 1970

Current service: With the US Navy and Marine Corps

Recognition: Long tapering fuselage with a short wide fin and swept tailplane either side of the tailcone. A wide cockpit canopy overlooks the short rounded nose which has a refuelling probe on top. The broad, slightly swept wings are set at mid-fuselage with the engine intakes below and forward of the wing roots. A large electronics pod is built into the top of the fin.

Variants: The original EA-6A, now retired, retained partial strike capability and had only two seats. The EA-6B has the latest ICAP-2 avionics and ALQ-99 tactical jamming system — it is now the USAF's principal ECM asset, though still operated by USN and USMC units.

Above and below: **Grumman EA-6 Prowlers are the principal ECM asset in the US Navy, US Marine Corps and USAF.** *PRM*

Grumman F-14 Tomcat

Twin-turbofan two-seat carrier-borne variable-geometry interceptor
Basic data for F-14D
Powerplant: Two General Electric F110-GE-400 turbofans of 16,000lb st (71.17kN) dry and 27,000lb st (120.1kN) with afterburner
Span: 64ft 1in (19.54m) wings spread
Length: 62ft 8in (19.10m)
Max speed: 1,238mph (1,997km/h)
Armament: One GE M-61A1 Vulcan 20mm multi-barrel cannon plus four under-fuselage and two under-wing hardpoints, carrying two AIM-54 Phoenix, AIM-7 Sparrows or AIM-9 Sidewinders.
First aircraft flown: 21 December 1970 (F-14A); September 1986 (F-14D)
Entered service: October 1972
Current service: With the US Navy
Recognition: Variable-geometry wings which form a delta shape with the all-moving tailplane in the fully-

Right and below: A US Navy Grumman F-14A Tomcat carrier-borne fighter. *PRM*

swept position. Angular intakes mounted at the wing roots below the long bubble canopy. Twin fins are mounted above the jetpipes of the engines. An arrester hook is positioned under the rear fuselage between two angular strakes.
Variants: The F-14A is the original version, which remains in service but is in the process of being upgraded. Some carry the Tactical Air Reconnaissance Pod System (TARPS). Following on was the F-14B, deployed from 1988 onwards (both converted and new-build aircraft), with the F110-GE-400 engine and avionics alterations, and then the F-14D (again a mixture of upgraded and new aircraft) incorporating digital avionics.

Hawker Siddeley/BAe 125

Above: Hawker Siddeley/BAe 125 in service with the RAF. *PRM*

Twin-engined navigation trainer, VIP/transport and SAR aircraft

Basic data for BAe 125 CC3

Powerplant: Two Garrett AiResearch TFE731-3-1H turbofans of 3,700lb st (16.48kN)
Span: 47ft 0in (14.33m)
Length: 50ft 8½in (15.46m)
Max speed: 502mph (808km/h)
Accommodation: Five or six passengers plus two/three crew (VIP)
First aircraft flown: 13 August 1962 (HS125 prototype); 21 January 1971 (Series 600); 28 June 1976 (Series 700).
Entered service: 1966 (RAF Dominie T1)
Current service: With the RAF and the air arms of Botswana, Brazil, Japan, Malawi, Saudi Arabia and South Africa.
Recognition: Low-swept wing, with square tips. Swept fin and rudder with extended dorsal fillet. Swept tailplane set high on fin. Short deep ventral strake at rear fuselage extremity. Pod-mounted engines on each side of fuselage. Six

fuselage windows on each side of fuselage with forward entry door on the RAF's CC3. This aircraft also has an infra-red countermeasures unit in the tail.
Variants: The Series 2 was a military version of the BAe 125-600 that had a lengthened fuselage with increased seating capacity. The Series 700 introduced Garrett AiResearch turbofans in place of the Viper turbojets, to achieve significant savings in fuel consumption and therefore increased range. Both the Series 600 and Series 700 have a longer fuselage than earlier versions of the type. The HS125 Series 2 was the basis for the RAF's Dominie T1 navigation trainer, that accommodates a flightcrew of two pilots, instructor and three student navigators. No 32 (The Royal) Squadron operates six BAe 125 CC3 jet transports in the VIP/rapid communications role. Now produced by Raytheon as the Hawker 800, 10 U-125As (Hawker 800s) have been delivered to the Japan Air Self Defence Force for SAR.

Hawker Siddeley Nimrod

Four-turbofan long-range maritime patrol and anti-submarine aircraft

Basic data for Nimrod MR2

Powerplant: Four Rolls-Royce Spey RB168-20 turbofans of 12,140lb st (54.0kN)

Span: 114ft 10in (35.00m)

Length: 126ft 9in (38.63m)

Max speed: 575mph (926km/h)

Armament: Internal bay for up to nine Stingray torpedoes, bombs, mines, depth charges and the Harpoon anti-ship missile. Sidewinder AAMs can be carried on underwing pylons.

Crew: 13

First aircraft flown: 23 May 1967 (MR1)

Entered service: 2 October 1969 (MR1); 23 August 1979 (MR2 redelivery)

Current service: With the RAF (three R1, 23 MR2)

Recognition: Resembles the DH106 Comet, from which it is derived. Long 'double bubble' fuselage

with the cockpit built into the steeply-raked nose. The fuselage tailcone extends well beyond the fin and rudder to house a magnetic anomaly detector (MAD) unit. The low-set wings are slightly swept on the forward edge. The four turbofans are buried in the inboard section of the wings. Bullet-shaped wing fairings project from the leading-edges towards the wingtips. The fin, which has a large dorsal section extending well forward, is surmounted by an elliptical-shaped fairing. All Nimrods have an in-flight refuelling probe projecting from the fuselage above the cockpit.

Variants: The only variants are the three electronic reconnaissance R1s, lacking the tail MAD extension, and the MR2 which is the standard MR/ASW version. Some 21 aircraft are to be rebuilt by FR Aviation and British Aerospace to Nimrod 2000 standard for the RAF, due for re-delivery between 2001 and 2006.

Below: **A Hawker Siddeley Nimrod MR2, the RAF's maritime reconnaissance and anti-submarine aircraft.** *APM*

Ilyushin Il-76 'Candid'

Four-turbofan medium/long-range transport aircraft

Basic data for Il-76MD 'Candid-B'

Powerplant: Four Aviadvigatel D-30KP-1 turbofans of 26,455lb st (117.7kN)

Span: 165ft 8in (50.50m)

Length: 152ft 10in (46.59m)

Max speed: 528mph (850km/h)

Armament: Can carry two 23mm cannon in the rear turret

Accommodation: Crew of seven; maximum payload of 88,183lb (40,000kg)

First aircraft flown: 25 March 1971

Entered service: 1974

Current service: With the Russian armed forces; also in Algeria, Belarus, Cuba, India, Iraq, Libya, North Korea, Syria and Ukraine.

Recognition: Circular wide-body fuselage with swept fin and rudder and 'T' tail. The swept wings are set on the top of the fuselage with the four engines hung in underwing pods. The main undercarriage retracts into fairings on the undersides of the fuselage. There is a small but distinctive ventral nose radome. Some 'Candid-B' versions feature a tail turret.

Variants: The original 'civil' Il-76T transport variant was redesignated Il-76TD with uprated engines, but retained the 'Candid-A' name; similarly, the military Il-76M became the Il-76MD but was still a 'Candid-B'. A tanker derivative, the Il-78M 'Midas', became operational in 1987 with refuelling pods beneath the outer wings and a hose reel unit in the rear fuselage. It now serves with Russia and the Ukraine, though the AAR equipment is not always carried by the latter's aircraft. The Russian AF also flies the A-50 'Mainstay' and Il-976 AEW variants, while Iraq has its own Il-76T AEW conversions known as the Adnan-1. Other variations on the basic design are an airborne command and control aircraft, and the Il-76DMP firefighter. The new Il-76MF is a stretched version with four Aviadvigatel PS-90AN turbofans of 35,275lb st (156.9kN).

Below: **The Ilyushin Il-76 'Candid' is in service as a transport aircraft with the Russian and other former Soviet air forces.** *PRM*

Kamov Ka-27/28/32 'Helix'

Shipboard anti-submarine warfare, assault transport and SAR helicopter

Basic data for Ka-27PL

Powerplant: Two Klimov (Isotov) TV3-117V turboshafts of 2,205eshp (1,645kW)

Rotor diameter: 52ft 2in (15.90m)

Fuselage length: 37ft 1in (11.30m)

Max speed: 155mph (250km/h)

Armament: Depth charges or torpedoes carried in ventral weapons bay

Crew: Three

First aircraft flown: 8 August 1973

Entered service: September 1978

Current service: With Russian Naval Aviation, plus India and Vietnam

Recognition: Deep and squat fuselage with coaxial contra-rotating twin main rotors mounted on a single shaft. Large twin fins and rudders without tail rotor. Twin engines mounted above cabin. A chin radome is prominent. Four-leg undercarriage with wheels.

Variants: The basic Ka-27PL 'Helix-A' ASW helicopter features an undernose-mounted search radar, dipping sonar and disposable sonobuoys; Ka-27PS 'Helix-D' is the SAR version, the Ka-27K is a further ASW variant and the Ka-28 is the export derivative of the basic 'Helix-A'. The ostensibly civil Ka-32 'Helix-C', available for flying crane, offshore support, rescue, maritime patrol and firefighting applications, is also used by the Russian Navy for SAR and ice reconnaissance.

Below: The Russian Navy operates the Ka-28 'Helix' for anti-submarine duties. *PRM*

Kamov Ka-50 Werewolf/'Hokum'

Twin-turbine close support helicopter
Basic data for Ka-50 'Hokum-A'
Powerplant: Two Klimov TV-3-117VK turboshafts of 2,190eshp (1,633kW)
Rotor diameter: 47ft 7in (14.50m)
Length: 52ft 6in (16.00m)
Max speed: 217mph (350km/h)
Armament: Single-barrel 30mm 2A42 gun on starboard side of fuselage. Two hardpoints on each stub wing which can carry up to 80 S-8 80mm air-to-surface rockets in B-8 packs, or up to 12 Vikhr (AT-12) tube-launched laser-guided air-to-surface missiles. Other options include gun pods and AAMs.
First aircraft flown: 27 July 1982
Entered service: 1996
Current service: Currently with Russian Army Aviation Centre only. Myanmar and Slovakia are possible export customers.

Recognition: Coaxial, contra-rotating and widely separated three-blade rotors, with swept blade tips. Small fuselage cross-section, with nose sensors. Flat-screen cockpit. Small sweptback tailfin, with inset rudder and large tab. High-set tailplane on rear fuselage, with endplate auxiliary fins and no tail rotor. Mid-set unswept wings, carrying ECM pods at tips and four underwing weapon pylons. Engines above wing roots, with prominent exhaust suppressors. Retractable tricycle-type landing gear, with twin-wheel nose unit and single mainwheels, which retract rearward, and all are semi-exposed when up.
Variants: Ka-50 'Hokum-A' — the basic single-seat version; Ka-50N — night attack helicopter; Ka-52 Alligator/'Hokum-B' — a two-seat side-by-side, combat-reconnaissance version.

Below: This Kamov Ka-50 'Hokum' is operated by the Russian Army as a single-seat close support helicopter. *PRM*

Lockheed C-5 Galaxy

Four-turbofan strategic transport
Basic data for C-5B
Powerplant: Four General Electric TF39-GE-1C turbofans of 43,000lb st (191.3kN)
Span: 222ft 8½in (67.88m)
Length: 247ft 10in (75.54m)
Max speed: 571mph (919km/h)
Accommodation: Crew of five; payload of over 261,000lb (118,385kg) such as three CH-47 Chinook helicopters or two M1A1 Abrams tanks, or 350 troops with 75 on the upper deck
First aircraft flown: 30 June 1968 (C-5A); 10 September 1985 (C-5B)
Entered service: 17 December 1969 (C-5A); 8 January 1986 (C-5B)
Current service: With the USAF

Recognition: Very large bulbous fuselage tapering towards the tail. Swept fin and rudder with a 'T' tailplane. Swept wings set on top of the fuselage with underslung podded engines projecting well forward of the leading-edge. Rear loading ramp from the fuselage floor. Multi-bogie main undercarriage retracts into fairings on the fuselage under the wings. High-set flightdeck above the short, rounded nose.
Variants: The existing C-5As (all re-winged in the 1980s) were joined from 1986 by new-build C-5Bs, with an improved wing, 20% increase in payload, new avionics and better fatigue resistance. Two C-5Cs are modified versions that can transport satellites and related space equipment.

Below: Lockheed's C-5B Galaxy, the West's largest transport aircraft. *PRM*

Lockheed C-141 StarLifter

Four-turbofan strategic transport aircraft
Basic data for C-141B
Powerplant: Four Pratt & Whitney TF33-7
turbofans of 21,000lb st (93.4kN)
Span: 159ft 11in (48.74m)
Length: 168ft 4in (51.31m)
Max speed: 564mph (908km/h)
Accommodation: Maximum cargo payload
94,508lb (42,868kg); crew of four plus 208
troops, 168 paratroops or 103 stretchers.
First aircraft flown: 17 December 1963
(C-141A); 24 March 1977
(C-141B)
Entered service: 1965 (C-141A);
4 December 1979 (C-141B)
Current service: With the USAF
Recognition: Long circular 'narrow-body'

fuselage with a swept fin and rudder and 'T' tail.
The swept wings are set on top of the fuselage
with the four engines hung in underwing pods.
Main undercarriage retracts into fairings on the
undersides of the fuselage. There is a small but
distinctive dorsal hump just behind the cockpit.
Variants: The original C-141A had a shorter
fuselage but by 1983 all but four StarLifters (the
exceptions being NC-141A testbeds) had been
converted to C-141Bs with a 23ft 4in (7.11m)
fuselage extension, avionics improvements and
other detailed modifications. Thirteen C-141Bs
are operated for special missions support, with
defensive countermeasures and a retractable FLIR
pod; 64 C-141Bs are being modified as C-141Cs,
incorporating a new glass cockpit.

Below: The USAF's long-serving strategic transport, the Lockheed C-141B StarLifter. *PRM*

Lockheed F-104 Starfighter

Single-turbojet all-weather strike and fighter aircraft

Basic data for F-104S/ASA

Powerplant: One General Electric J79-GE-19 turbojet of 11,870lb st (52.8kN) dry and 17,900lb st (79.6kN) with afterburner

Span: 21ft 11in (6.68m)

Length: 54ft 9in (16.69m)

Max speed: 1,450mph (2,330km/h)

Armament: Up to 7,500lb external stores on pylons including Sparrow III or Aspide air-to-air missiles; a 20mm Vulcan cannon can also be carried, along with wingtip-mounted AIM-9L Sidewinders.

First aircraft flown: 28 February 1954 (F-104A); December 1968 (F-104S)

Entered service: 26 January 1958 (F-104A); 1969 (F-104S)

Current service: With the Italian AF

Recognition: Long 'pencil' fuselage with a small 'T' tail mounted over and behind the large jetpipe. Very short stubby thin wings with marked anhedral set into the fuselage sides, with engine air intakes at the wing roots. Sharp pointed nose with a streamlined cockpit canopy. The undercarriage retracts into the fuselage.

Variants: The F-104A and C were USAF fighter variants; the F-104B and D, corresponding two-seat combat trainers. The F-104G and similar CF-104 and F-104J were strike fighters; the TF-104G was an improved trainer and two-seat reconnaissance aircraft. The F-104S, built by Aeritalia, was the final production aircraft with a more powerful J79 turbojet for the interceptor role. The Italian AF has upgraded its single-seat Starfighters to F-104S/ASA standard, with FIAR Setter radar and Selenia Aspide compatibility — they will remain in service until Eurofighter 2000's arrival.

Below: **A small number of Lockheed F-104 Starfighters remain in service with the Italian AF.**
PRM

Lockheed F-117A Nighthawk

Twin-turbofan single-seat 'stealth' strike aircraft
Basic data for F-117A
Powerplant: Two General Electric F404-GE-F1D2 non-afterburning turbofans of 10,800lb st (48.0kN)
Span: 43ft 3in (13.20m)
Length: 65ft 11in (20.08m)
Max speed: 646mph (1,040km/h)
Armament: GBU-27 or GBU-27 Paveway LGBs carried in internal weapons bay, plus conventional bombs of up to 2,000lb (907kg) weight each, typically GBU-10 and GBU-27, up to a maximum load of 5,000lb (2,268kg). Tactical munitions dispensers and missiles including Maverick or HARM can also be used, along with Sidewinders for self-defence. New weapons include GBU-30s (JDAM) and JSOW.

First aircraft flown: 18 June 1981
Entered service: 23 August 1982
Current service: Only with the USAF (53 now on strength), last aircraft delivered 12 July 1990.
Recognition: A unique multi-faceted (angled flat surfaces) shape to minimise radar returns. Shield slot exhausts designed to dissipate heat emissions. Highly swept wing leading-edges, W-shaped trailing-edge, straight wingtips, an integrated fuselage and a V-shaped tailplane comprising upper section slab 'ruddervators' that combine the functions of rudders and elevators. Engine gases mix with bypass air and exit through platypus exhausts to reduce the IR signature.
Variants: Upgrades of the F-117A fleet continue, with Phase V completed in March 1997.

Below: Examples of the Lockheed F-117A Nighthawk saw service in the Gulf War. *DJM*

Lockheed P-3 Orion

Four-turboprop anti-submarine warfare and maritime patrol aircraft

Basic data for P-3C

Powerplant: Four Allison T56-A-14 turboprops of 4,910eshp (3,660kW)

Span: 99ft 8in (30.37m)

Length: 116ft 10in (35.61m)

Max speed: 471mph (760km/h)

Armament: Ten underwing hardpoints can carry eight AGM-84 Harpoons, 10 torpedoes or 10 depth bombs or rockets. Eight torpedoes or depth bombs can be accommodated in the internal weapons bay.

Crew: 10

First aircraft flown: 25 November 1959 (P-3A); 18 September 1968 (P-3C)

Entered service: 13 August 1962 (P-3A); July 1970 (P-3C)

Current service: With the armed forces of Australia, Canada, Chile, Greece, Iran, Japan, Netherlands, New Zealand, Norway, Portugal, South Korea, Spain, Thailand and the USA.

Recognition: Four turboprops widely spaced on the broad-chord short-span square-tipped wings. A circular-section fuselage mounted above the wing. Curved shape fin and rudder with a forward dorsal extension. Tailplane set on top of the rear fuselage below the fin and rudder. Rounded nose with small cockpit windows above. The distinctive MAD probe extends from the tailcone.

Variants: The original P-3A was developed from a civil airliner, the L-188 Electra. The P-3B had more powerful engines and other refinements, while the P-3C featured a major avionics upgrade (further updates having followed since). With the USN, the WP-3D is equipped for weather reconnaissance and the EP-3E is a special mission electronic surveillance variant, while various early aircraft have been converted to UP/VP-3 derivatives for utility/VIP transport. The Canadian Forces have the CP-140 Aurora with special systems. Lockheed production has ceased although P-3C manufacture continues in Japan, as the Kawasaki EP-3. The latest US Navy P-3Cs are the Update III aircraft, incorporating additional system enhancements.

Below: **This Lockheed P-3 Orion is operated by the Royal Netherlands Navy for maritime patrol duties.** *APM*

Lockheed S-3 Viking

Twin-turbofan four-seat carrier-borne anti-submarine aircraft
Basic data for S-3B
Powerplant: Two General Electric TF-34-GE-400A/B turbofans of 9,275lb st (41.3kN)
Span: 68ft 8in (20.93m)
Length: 53ft 4in (16.26m)
Max speed: 505mph (815km/h)
Armament: An internal, split, weapons bay can carry bombs, depth bombs, mines or torpedoes. There are two underwing pylons for AGM-84 Harpoon missiles, rocket pods, bombs, mines or flare launchers.
Crew: Four
First aircraft flown: 21 January 1972 (S-3A); September 1984 (S-3B)
Entered service: 20 February 1974 (S-3A)

Current service: With the US Navy
Recognition: Short stubby fuselage with a large swept fin and rudder. Swept wings are set on top of the fuselage with the engines hung on pylons beneath the leading-edge. The flightdeck is situated well forward with large windows overlooking the short rounded nose.
Variants: The S-3A fleet has been upgraded with improved electronic systems and the capability to carry the Harpoon air-to-surface missile as the S-3B. The US-3A is a COD (carrier on-board delivery) variant, while the ES-3A (that first flew in 1991) is an ELINT-gathering version which replaced the EA-3B Skywarrior. It features EW equipment in a dorsal fairing, a new radome, direction-finding antennae and an array of further antennae beneath the fuselage.

Below: The US Navy's Lockheed S-3A Viking carrier-borne anti-submarine aircraft. *PRM*

Lockheed Tristar

Three-turbofan tanker/transport aircraft
Basic data for Tristar K1/KC1
Powerplant: Three Rolls-Royce RB211-524B
turbofans of 50,000lb st (222.4kN)
Span: 164ft 4in (50.08m)
Length: 164ft 3in (50.06m)
Max speed: 605mph (973km/h)
Accommodation: Three crew plus up to 300
passengers; 100,060lb (45,387kg) of fuel for
transfer in flight
First aircraft flown: 17 November 1970 (L-1011);
9 July 1985 (first RAF K1)
Entered service: 1985 (K1)
Current service: With the RAF as a tanker and
heavy transport aircraft (two K1, four KC1, two
C2 and one C2A).

Recognition: Two engines in underwing nacelles
and one engine mounted on top of the fuselage
forward of the swept fin, with the jet efflux below
the rudder through the tail cone. Circular wide-
body fuselage with low-set swept wings at midway
point. Swept tailplane low-set either side of the
rear fuselage below the fin.
Variants: All of the RAF's Tristars are converted
ex-airline L-1011-500s — first to be delivered were
K1 tanker/transports, followed by the KC1s with a
large port side freight door. Pure cargo versions
are the C2 and C2A, the former without AAR
probes, and the latter incorporating new military
avionics.

Below: **Lockheed Tristars are used for strategic air-to-air refuelling and long-range transport
duties.** *DJM*

Lockheed U-2

Single-turbojet high-altitude electronic and optical reconnaissance aircraft

Basic data for U-2S

Powerplant: One General Electric F101-GE-F29 turbofan of 18,500lb st (83.9kN)

Span: 103ft 0in (31.39m)

Length: 63ft 0in (19.20m)

Max speed: 495mph (797km/h)

First aircraft flown: 1 August 1955 (U-2A)

Entered service: 1956 (U-2A); 28 October 1994 (U-2S)

Current service: With the USAF

Recognition: Long circular-section fuselage with tall narrow-chord fin. Semicircular intakes either side of the fuselage between wing leading-edge and cockpit. High-aspect ratio wings carrying large sensing pods beneath them.

Variants: Originally built as the U-2A, a more powerful engine gave rise to the U-2B. Some U-2Bs were modified for the ELINT role, being redesignated U-2C. The production line was reopened in 1968 to produce the U-2R with both increased span and length. An acknowledgement of the aircraft's true role came with the TR-1A, a similar version to the U-2R featuring increased internal fuel and a tactical reconnaissance role — these new aircraft were redesignated as U-2Rs in 1992. All of the active fleet is now the re-engined U-2S, with a 15% increase in endurance, and a higher operational ceiling. Sensors are carried in detachable nose fittings, in the forward fuselage and underwing pods. Some aircraft carry Senior Span satellite communications equipment for data transmission in a teardrop-shaped dorsal-mounted pod. The conversion trainer is the U-2S(T), with a second cockpit above and to the rear of the normal pilot's position. A one-off version designated ER-2 was supplied to NASA.

Below: **Lockheed's U-2 is used by the USAF for high-level reconnaissance work.** *PRM*

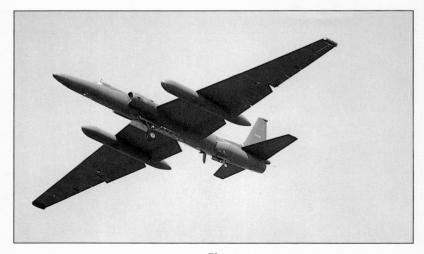

Lockheed Martin C-130 Hercules

Four-turboprop tactical transport and special missions aircraft

Basic data for C-130H

Powerplant: Four Allison T56-A-15 turboprops of 4,508eshp (3,362kW)

Span: 132ft 7in (40.41m)

Length: 97ft 9in (29.79m)

Max speed: 374mph (602km/h)

Accommodation: Crew of four or six and up to 92 troops, 64 paratroops or 74 stretchers; maximum payload of 42,675lb (19,355kg).

First aircraft flown: 23 August 1954 (YC-130); November 1964 (C-130H)

Entered service: 9 December 1956 (C-130A); March 1965 (C-130H)

Current service: With many of the world's air forces; by 1998, over 2,100 had been sold, of which over 1,000 are in service in the USA, Canada and South America.

Recognition: Four turboprops located under the high-set straight wing. A circular fuselage with a distinctive nose radome, undercarriage fairings and unswept tail for rear cargo loading. Tall shaped fin and rudder with a small dorsal extension forward of the fin. Tailplane at the extremity of the fuselage at the base of the fin and rudder. Few cabin windows.

Variants: One of the most successful military aircraft of all time, the C-130 Hercules has been developed for countless roles and countries. The standard transport C-130E and C-130H are the most numerically common sub-types, while the stretched version (most regularly the C-130H-30) is some 15ft (4.58m) longer. The civilian L-100 derivative is also used by some air arms. Other roles for which versions have been built or converted include air-to-air refuelling (USMC KC-130s, USAF MC-130Ps and Canadian CC-130Hs being among those thus equipped); weather reconnaissance (the USAF's WC-130, and DERA's unique Hercules W2); maritime patrol (C-130H-MPs, purchased by Indonesia and Malaysia); gunship (the AC-130 Spectre, the latest being the AC-130U); special electronic missions (the best-known being various USAF EC-130 sub-types); long-range SAR (the US Coast Guard's HC-130s, and USAF HC/MC-130Ps); Antarctic operations (ski-equipped LC-130s); and dedicated US Special Forces support (MC-130E/H). The latest C-130J, with an updated 'glass' cockpit and more powerful Allison T56 Series IV turboprops with six-blade propellers, entered service in 1998/9 with the USAF, USMC, RAF, Australia and Italy as confirmed customers.

Below: **The Lockheed C-130 Hercules, one of the most successful military transport of all time, seen here in RAF service.** *DJM*

Lockheed Martin (General Dynamics) F-16 Fighting Falcon

Single-turbofan, single-seat fighter/strike aircraft
Basic data for F-16C
Powerplant: One Pratt & Whitney F-100-PW-200/220/229 turbofan of 23,770lb st (105.74kN) with afterburner
Span: 32ft 9½in (10.0m) over wingtip missiles
Length: 49ft 4in (15.03m)
Max speed: 1,330mph (2,140km/h)
Armament: One M61A1 Vulcan 20mm rotary cannon; nine hardpoints (six underwing, one centreline and two wingtip) can carry up to 12,000lb (5,435kg) of ordnance. Weapons include AIM-9 Sidewinder or AIM-120 AMRAAM AAMs (on wingtip pylons), rockets, AGM-65 Maverick ASMs, Penguin anti-shipping missiles, bombs (among them GBU-10 and GBU-12 laser-guided weapons). AGM-88 HARM anti-radiation missiles can be used by later block-number aircraft.
First aircraft flown: 20 January 1974 (YF-16); 16 June 1984 (F-16C)
Entered service: 6 January 1979 (F-16A)
Current service: With the USAF and the air forces of Bahrain, Belgium, Denmark, Egypt, Greece, Indonesia, Israel, Jordan, Netherlands, Norway, Pakistan, Portugal, Singapore, South Korea, Taiwan, Thailand, Turkey and Venezuela.
Recognition: Large air intake beneath the fuselage. Pronounced single-piece bubble cockpit canopy. Front fuselage strakes extending into the short-span swept wings. Two large ventral strakes forward of the mid-fuselage-mounted tailplane. A swept angular fin with the jetpipe extending beyond the rudder trailing-edge.

Variants: The F-16A is the original single-seat production version (some being the modified Air Defense Fighter derivative, with a radar upgrade for this purpose); the two-seat version is the F-16B. The F-16C and F-16D are corresponding improved variants featuring the APG-68 updated radar, CRT cockpit and improved weapons capability — later block-number aircraft have incorporated a number of significant improvements including a night attack capability with LANTIRN pods, new radars and avionics, and powerplant changes. Mid-life update (MLU) programmes are in progress for various European F-16 operators, and several earlier USAF F-16C/Ds are being modified for close air support and battlefield interdiction.

Above and below: **Lockheed Martin F-16 Fighting Falcons are operated by many air arms around the world as a front-line single-seat strike aircraft.** *PRM*

LTV A-7 Corsair II

Single-turbofan single-seat attack aircraft
Basic data for A-7P
Powerplant: One Allison TF41-A-1 turbofan of 15,000lb st (66.7kN)
Span: 38ft 9in (11.80m)
Length: 46ft 0½in (14.06m)
Max speed: 698mph (1,123km/h)
Armament: One M61A1 Vulcan 20mm multi-barrel cannon and up to 15,000lb (6,805kg) of ordnance. Weapons options include AIM-9 Sidewinders, bombs (including laser-guided ordnance), AGM-65 Maverick ASMs, and rockets.
First aircraft flown: 27 September 1965 (A-7A); 26 September 1968 (A-7D)
Entered service: February 1967 (A-7A)
Current service: With the air forces of Greece, Portugal and Thailand.
Recognition: Long rectangular section fuselage with a large swept fin. The swept wings are shoulder-mounted and have six underwing pylons for stores. The cockpit is situated right at the nose with only the AN/APQ126 radar cone projecting forward and above the large oval engine intake. The swept tailplane is set on the sides of the rear fuselage.
Variants: The original US Navy A-7A was subsequently replaced by the more powerful A-7B, while the re-engined A-7D with improved avionics was adopted by the USAF (later joined by the A-7K two-seater). The US Navy's A-7C and A-7E were further developments. Portuguese AF aircraft, designated A-7P and TA-7P, are rebuilt A-7A/Bs while those of Greece, A-7Hs and TA-7Hs, are based on the A-7E. The Royal Thai Navy operates surplus USN A-7Es.

Below: **A Portuguese Air Force LTV A-7P Corsair II.** *PRM*

McDonnell Douglas A-4 Skyhawk

Single-turbojet single-seat land-based or carrier-borne attack aircraft

Basic data for A-4M

Powerplant: One Pratt & Whitney J52-P-408A turbojet of 11,200lb st (50.0kN)

Span: 27ft 6in (8.38m)

Length: 40ft 3¼in (12.27m)

Max speed: 645mph (1,038km/h)

Armament: Two 20mm Colt Mk 12 cannon in wing roots, plus five hardpoints for up to 9,155lb (4,155kg) of ordnance. Weapons include bombs, cluster bombs, AIM-9 Sidewinders, Bullpup and Maverick ASMs.

First aircraft flown: 22 June 1954

Entered service: October 1956

Current service: With the US Navy, and also the air forces of Argentina, Indonesia, Israel, Kuwait, Malaysia, New Zealand and Singapore.

Recognition: Very small, compact aircraft with a short fuselage; cockpit well forward, and a 'humped' fuselage behind the cockpit in the latest versions. The wing is delta-shaped and low-set. The tall fin is swept on the forward edge, with the triangular tailplane at its base.

Variants: The single-seat Skyhawk has progressed through a number of variants: the A-4F in 1966 introduced the 'camel hump' avionics saddle behind the cockpit; the A-4M in 1970 was an improved USMC variant; and the A-4N Skyhawk II was a further enhanced version for Israel. The two-seat TA-4E introduced in 1965 had a lengthened fuselage, tandem cockpit and more powerful engine. Subsequent TA-4 variants have been similar except for Singapore's TA-4S which has two separate cockpits. Only two-seat TA-4Fs used by the USN as advanced trainers survive in US service and are soon to be withdrawn. New Zealand's A-4Ks have been upgraded and can carry AIM-9L Sidewinders, AGM-65 Mavericks and LGBs.

Below: **McDonnell Douglas A-4 Skyhawks remain in service with the US Navy and US Marine Corps.** *PRM*

McDonnell Douglas AV-8 Harrier II

Single-turbofan single-seat V/STOL ground-attack aircraft

Basic data for AV-8B

Powerplant: One Rolls-Royce F402-RR-408 (Pegasus 11-61) vectored-thrust turbofan of 23,800lb st (105.9kN)

Span: 30ft 4in (9.25m)

Length: 46ft 4in (14.12m)

Max speed: 660mph (1,065km/h)

Armament: One GE GAU-12/A 25mm rotary cannon or two 30mm Aden cannon; plus seven pylons for 9,200lb (4,173kg) of ordnance.

First aircraft flown: 26 February 1981 (AV-8B)

Entered service: January 1984 (AV-8B); July 1993 (AV-8B Harrier II Plus)

Current service: With the US Marine Corps, and the Italian and Spanish navies.

Recognition: Large semicircular engine intakes on either side of the fuselage forward of the wing. A high-set cockpit over the short pointed nose. Broad-chord wing with root extensions and marked anhedral, mounted on top of the fuselage. The fin is swept on the forward edge with a ventral fillet. The swivelling jet efflux nozzles are situated on the fuselage sides below the wings. The main undercarriage is located under the fuselage with outriggers which retract into wing pods.

Variants: The AV-8B was developed from the earlier AV-8A. It has an improved super-critical wing of composite construction with extended wing roots, new engine nozzles, larger flaps and other refinements. The ultimate development is the AV-8B Harrier II Plus, which entered USMC service in July 1993. It is fitted with the multi-mode Hughes APG-65 radar, giving AIM-120, AIM-7 and AGM-84 compatibility, and has a 17in longer fuselage than the previous version together with bigger LERX (leading-edge root extensions). A total of 114 AV-8Bs are being upgraded to Plus standard, together with 24 new production examples. The two-seat version is the TAV-8B.

Below: **The latest McDonnell Douglas AV-8 Harrier II is flown by the US Marine Corps.** *PRM*

McDonnell Douglas DC-9/C-9 Nightingale

Twin-turbofan aeromedical/transport

Basic data for C-9A/DC-9-30

Powerplant: Two Pratt & Whitney JT8D-9 turbofans of 14,500lb st (64.5kN)

Span: 93ft 5in (28.47m)

Length: 119ft 3½in (36.37m)

Max speed: 580mph (935km/h)

Accommodation: Two crew and up to 40 stretchers or 115 passengers

First aircraft flown:
25 February 1965 (DC-9-10);
8 August 1968 (C-9A)

Entered service: 10 August 1968 (C-9A)

Current service: With the USAF (C-9A/C), US Navy and Marine Corps (DC-9-31/C-9B Skytrain II) and the Kuwait and Italian air forces.

Recognition: Engines mounted on the sides of the rear fuselage forward of the fin. Low-set swept wings which taper towards the wingtips. Narrow-body, circular fuselage with a rounded nose and pointed tail. Angular swept fin and rudder with a swept 'T' tailplane mounted near the top. A small rounded fin extension above the tailplane with a bullet fairing to the rear.

Variants: Military operators of the DC-9 have used the Series 30 airframe for specialist aeromedical, VIP and general transport work. The USAF's aeromedical C-9A Nightingales are the most numerous, three C-9Cs also serving as VIP/staff transports. In US Navy service, the C-9B Skytrain II is used for fleet logistics support (two also being flown by the USMC), augmented by 10 further aircraft known simply as DC-9-31s. The air forces of Kuwait and Italy also use the DC-9-32.

Below: **A McDonnell Douglas C-9 Nightingale used by the USAF for transport and air ambulance purposes.** *PRM*

McDonnell Douglas/Boeing C-17 Globemaster III

Long-range and intra-theatre heavy cargo transport
Basic data for C-17A
Powerplant: Four Pratt & Whitney F117-PW-100 turbofans of 40,700lb st (181.25kN), each fitted with directed-flow thrust reversers deployable both in flight and on the ground.
Span: 169ft 10in (51.76m) over winglets
Length: 174ft 0in (53.04m)
Max cruising speed: 403mph (648km/h)
Accommodation: Flightcrew of two, plus loadmaster; 100 passengers on seating pallets, 48 stretcher patients, or 75 troops on temporary fuselage side and centreline seats, or 102 paratroops.
First aircraft flown: 15 September 1991
Entered service: 14 June 1993
Current service: US Air Force. Original requirement was for 210, cut to 120 in 1991 and at present capped at 80.

Recognition: High-mounted swept wing with 9½ft high winglets. Externally blown flap system — with extended flaps in exhaust flow from engines during take-off and landing giving STOL performance. Engines pylon-mounted in individual underwing pods. Supercritical wing with 25° sweepback. Four underwing pods on trailing-edge of each wing. Bulbous circular fuselage. Main undercarriage retracts into fairings on the undersides of the fuselage. Rear-loading ramp. Upper fuselage line rises to large swept fin with T-tail. Small strakes under tail. Mainwheel undercarriage units, each consisting of two legs in tandem, with three wheels on each leg. Voluminous cargo hold capable of accommodating attack helicopters and the M1 Abrams battle tank. Paratroop door at rear on each side.
Variants: Export version is under development.

Below: **The USAF's latest long-range and intra-theatre heavy cargo transport is the McDonnell Douglas C-17 Globemaster III.** *PRM*

McDonnell Douglas F-4 Phantom II

Twin-turbojet two-seat fighter and multi-mission aircraft

Basic data for F-4E

Powerplant: Two Pratt & Whitney J79-GE-17A turbojets of 11,810lb st (52.5kN) dry and 17,900lb st (79.6kN) with afterburner

Span: 38ft 8in (11.77m)

Length: 63ft 0in (19.20m)

Max speed: 1,481mph (2,390km/h)

Armament: A wide range including four Sparrow and four AIM-9 Sidewinder AAMs or up to 16,000lb (7,250kg) of ordnance, and a 20mm M61A1 Vulcan rotary cannon.

First aircraft flown: 27 May 1958 (YF4H-1); 30 June 1967 (F-4E)

Entered service: December 1960 (F-4A); October 1967 (F-4E)

Current service: With the armed forces of Egypt, Germany, Greece, Iran, Israel, Japan, South Korea, Spain and Turkey, and used by the US forces for trials and as drones.

Recognition: A long fuselage with a cutaway section beneath the swept square-topped fin. The low-set broad-chord wings are well swept on the forward edge with a marked dihedral in the outer section. The narrow engine intakes are located either side of the forward fuselage below the long streamlined cockpit. The jetpipes emerge from the fuselage just aft of the wings, forward of the anhedralled tailplane.

Variants: The original F-4A was replaced by the more powerful and improved F-4B for the USN and the USAF's F-4C. Reconnaissance versions of these feature lengthened noses to house cameras. Further equipment updates produced the F-4D, and the F-4E with a fixed nose-mounted cannon (developed into the reconnaissance RF-4E). The Luftwaffe's F-4F also had aerodynamic improvements including leading-edge slats. Specially developed for 'Wild Weasel' attack, the F-4G had a further equipment/electronic update while the F-4J/S was the final improved USN variant. IAI is upgrading Israeli F-4Es to Kurnass 2000 status with improved avionics, along with Turkish aircraft, while Japan's F-4EJs are being updated to F-4EJ Kai standard with a Westinghouse APG-66J radar. Germany's Improved Combat Efficiency (ICE) programme adds a Hughes APG-65 radar and AIM-20 AMRAAM compatibility to its F-4F fleet. All Phantoms have now been retired from service with the US forces, but a large number of surplus USAF and USN machines that have been retained in storage have been and are being converted by Tracor to QF-4 drones.

Below: **McDonnell Douglas Phantoms still serve with the German Air Force as an air defence fighter.** *PRM*

McDonnell Douglas/Boeing F-15 Eagle

Twin-turbofan single-seat air superiority fighter

Basic data for F-15C

Powerplant: Two Pratt & Whitney F100-PW-220 turbofans of 14,670lb st (65.3kN) dry and 23,770lb st (105.7kN) with afterburner

Span: 42ft 10in (13.05m)

Length: 63ft 10in (19.45m)

Max speed: 1,650mph (2,655km/h)

Armament: One 20mm M61A1 Vulcan rotary cannon, four AIM-7 Sparrow air-to-air missiles, four AIM-9 Sidewinder and AIM-120 air-to-air missiles and five hardpoints for up to 16,000lb (7,273kg) of ordnance.

First aircraft flown: 27 July 1972 (YF-15A); 27 February 1979 (F-15C)

Entered service: 14 November 1974 (F-15A); September 1979 (F-15C)

Current service: With the USAF and in Israel, Japan and Saudi Arabia.

Recognition: A long nose with raised canopy; angular intakes at the wing roots. The shoulder-mounted wings have a sharp leading-edge sweep but little trailing-edge sweep. The widely-spaced twin fins are square-topped with a small fillet extending along the top of the rear fuselage. The all-moving tailplane has its trailing-edge well aft of the jetpipe line.

Variants: The F-15A was the original version with the F-15B as a two-seat operational trainer. These have subsequently largely been replaced in front-line service by the F-15C and F-15D respectively. These variants feature an increased fuel capacity (by means of conformal tanks) and improved avionics. The MSIP (Multi-Stage Improvement Program) update, on all four of these sub-types, has added numerous improvements including radar upgrades.

Below: The USAF's McDonnell Douglas F-15C Eagle air defence fighter. *DJM*

McDonnell Douglas/Boeing F-15E Strike Eagle

Twin-turbofan two-seat multi-role strike/attack aircraft
Basic data for F-15E
Powerplant: Two Pratt & Whitney F100-PW-229 turbofans of 17,800lb st (79.18kN) dry and 29,100lb st (129.45kN) with afterburner
Span: 42ft 9¾in (13.05m)
Length: 63ft 9in (19.43m)
Max speed: 1,650mph (2,655km/h)
Armament: Up to 24,250lb (11,000kg) of ordnance can be carried externally. Weapons include GBU-10/12/15 LGBs, cluster bombs, the AGM-65 Maverick and Mk 82 or Mk 84 bombs, plus AGM-88 HARMs for defence suppression, AIM-7 Sparrows and AIM-120 AMRAAMs, and AIM-9 Sidewinder AAMs. A 20mm six-barrelled M61A1 Vulcan cannon is also carried.
First aircraft flown: 8 July 1980 (Strike Eagle prototype); 11 December 1986 (F-15E)
Entered service: 29 December 1988 (F-15E)

Current service: F-15E serves with USAF only; F-15I for Israel, F-15S for Saudi Arabia.
Recognition: No great changes to the standard F-15 appearance — two-seat configuration gives a slightly hump-backed appearance, with a more drooping nose than other two-seat Eagles. Large conformal fuel tanks with weapons points attached make for a fatter frontal appearance around the engine intakes when viewed head-on.
Variants: The F-15E Strike Eagle is the two-seat all-weather interdictor/strike derivative of the basic Eagle, having an improved weapons load capacity compared to standard F-15s and the LANTIRN night nav/attack system. Higher-powered F100-PW-229 turbofans have been fitted to F-15Es from August 1991. Based on the Strike Eagle, the Royal Saudi AF now operates the F-15S version with systems differences, and Israel the similar F-15I (locally named Thunder), both alongside C and D models

Below: Two-seat strike/attack aircraft, the McDonnell Douglas F-15E Strike Eagle was developed from the F-15 Eagle fighter. *DJM*

McDonnell Douglas/Boeing F/A-18 Hornet

Twin-turbofan single-seat carrier-borne or land-based fighter/attack aircraft
Basic data for F/A-18C
Powerplant: Two General Electric F404-GE-402EPE turbofans of 17,700lb st (78.7kN) with afterburner
Span: 37ft 6in (11.43m)
Length: 56ft 0in (17.07m)
Max speed: 1,190mph (1,910km/h)
Armament: One 20mm M61A1 Vulcan rotary cannon and a variety of air-to-air missiles or ordnance up to 15,500lb (7,030kg). Missiles are normally carried on the wingtips.
First aircraft flown: 18 November 1978 (F/A-18A); 3 September 1986 (F/A-18C)
Entered service: May 1980 (F/A-18A); 1987 (F/A-18C)
Current service: With the US Navy and Marine Corps, together with the air forces of Australia, Canada, Finland, Kuwait, Malaysia, South Korea, Spain and Switzerland.
Recognition: Long fuselage with a distinctive humped back. The twin fins are set at 30° and mounted well forward of the jetpipes, while the tailplanes are set either side at the rear. A

clearview bubble canopy overlooks the long tapered nose. The broad-chord wings have a slight leading-edge sweep and an extending fillet forward to the cockpit. Engine intakes are either side of the lower fuselage under the wings.
Variants: The single-seat F/A-18A and corresponding two-seat F/A-18B were the initial production versions, followed by the improved F/A-18C and D. These newer machines incorporate better weapons delivery, APG-73 radar and AIM-120 AMRAAM compatibility, self-protection jamming capability and many other refinements. All-weather night attack capability was to follow on later C and D models for the USN and USMC. Canada operates single- and two-seat CF-188s, and Spain the EF/A-18 (both local designations). The next-generation Hornet will be the F/A-18E and F, now in the throes of test and development flying — these have a longer fuselage, increased wingspan and wing area, and larger tailfins, while the powerplant is the F414-GE-400 engine which offers major performance enhancements, and radar systems have been improved.

Below: **McDonnell Douglas F/A-18C Hornet attack/fighters serve with the Swiss Air Force.** *PRM*

McDonnell Douglas KC-10 Extender/KDC-10

Three-turbofan long-range strategic transport/tanker
Basic data for KC-10A
Powerplant: Three General Electric F103-GE-100 turbofans of 52,500lb st (233.5kN)
Span: 165ft 5in (50.42m)
Length: 181ft 7in (55.35m)
Max speed: 595mph (957km/h)
Accommodation: Up to 75 personnel plus 200,000lb (90,718kg) transferable fuel or 169,409lb (76,842kg) maximum cargo payload
First aircraft flown: 29 August 1970 (DC-10); 12 July 1980 (KC-10A)
Entered service: 17 March 1981 (KC-10A)
Current service: The USAF is the sole KC-10

operator, while the Netherlands use the KDC-10.
Recognition: Two engines in underwing nacelles close to the fuselage, and one engine mounted on the fin above the fuselage with a straight-through exhaust pipe to the rear. A circular, wide-body fuselage with low-set swept wings. Tailplane mid-set on the rear fuselage below the fin. Refuelling boom carried beneath the tailplane.
Variants: The KC-10A Extender is a military derivative of the civilian DC-10-30CF and is the only version currently in USAF service. However, since 1995 the Royal Netherlands AF has operated two KDC-10s, these being converted ex-Martinair DC-10-30CFs with an advanced new remote-control refuelling boom system.

Below: McDonnell Douglas KC-10As are the USAF's strategic transport and refuelling version of the DC-10. *PRM*

Mikoyan MiG-21 'Fishbed'

Single-turbojet single-seat fighter aircraft
Basic data for MiG-21MF 'Fishbed-J'
Powerplant: One MNPK Tumansky R-13-300 turbojet of 8,972lb st (39.92kN) dry and 14,307lb st (63.66kN) with afterburner
Span: 23ft 4¾in (7.15m)

Length: 51ft 8½in (15.76m) including probe
Max speed: 1,385mph (2,230km/h)
Armament: Four underwing pylons for AAMs on MiG-21MF, including AA-2 'Atoll' and AA-8 'Aphid'; type can also carry two each of 250kg or 500kg bombs, and four rocket pods

First aircraft flown: June 1956 (Ye-5 prototype); 20 May 1958 (MiG-21)
Entered service: December 1958 (MiG-21)
Current service: With the air arms of Afghanistan, Albania, Angola, Azerbaijan, Bangladesh, Bulgaria, Burkina Faso, Congo, Croatia, Cuba, Czech Republic, Ethiopia, Finland, Guinea Republic, Hungary, India, Iraq, Kazakhstan, Mali, Mongolia, Mozambique, Nigeria, North Korea, Poland, Romania, Slovakia, Sudan, Syria, Ukraine, Vietnam, Yemen and Zambia.
Recognition: Circular-section fuselage with a distinctive cone-shaped nose radome and lengthy pitot probe on top of nose. Small cockpit canopy on single-seaters blended into dorsal fuselage spine, bulged behind cockpit but which narrows towards the tail. Angular fin and rudder, and wings of delta configuration.
Variants: MiG-21F-13 'Fishbed-C' was first production aircraft, followed by MiG-21P 'Fishbed-D' with a modified fuselage and the MiG-21PF equipped with improved R-11F2-300 engines and radar. MiG-21PFM introduced the R-11F2S-300 engine and RS-2US missile compatibility. First of the progressively heavier, more sophisticated variants was the MiG-21R 'Fishbed-H' for reconnaissance; MiG-21SM was fitted with a fixed belly cannon, and the MiG-21MF 'Fishbed-J' again brought in more

powerful engines, and full AAM capability. MiG-21bis 'Fishbed-L/N' developed as a multi-role derivative with increased ground attack capability and greater fuel capacity. Two-seat versions are designated MiG-21U/US/UM 'Mongol'. Various MiG-21 upgrades are being planned, two being those by IAI/Elbit who are upgrading Romania's aircraft to MiG-21MF Lancer standard, and MIG-MAPO's MiG-21-93 which is that adopted by India.

Below: A Mikoyan MiG-21UM of the Czech Air Force. *PRM*

Mikoyan MiG-23/27 'Flogger'

Single-turbojet variable-geometry strike/fighter aircraft
Basic data for MiG-23ML 'Flogger-G'
Powerplant: One Soyuz Tumansky R-35-300 turbojet of 18,849lb st (83.88kN) dry and 28,660lb st (127.5kN) with afterburner
Span: 25ft 6½in (7.78m) wings spread
Length: 51ft 3¾in (15.65m)
Max speed: 1,553mph (2,500km/h)
Armament: Various AAMs such as the R-60 (AA-8 'Aphid') on air defence versions; other stores can include the R-23 (AA-7 'Apex') radar-homing missile, guided ASMs, rockets, bomblet dispensers and standard bombs. All aircraft carry a 23mm twin-barrelled GSh-23L cannon.
First aircraft flown: April 1967 (MiG-23); 1972 (MiG-27)
Entered service: 1969 (MiG-23); 1973 (MiG-27)
Current service: With the Russian air arms; also

in Afghanistan, Algeria, Angola, Belarus, Bulgaria, Cuba, Czech Republic, Ethiopia, India, Kazakhstan, Libya, North Korea, Poland, Romania, Sudan, Syria, Ukraine, Uzbekistan, Vietnam and Yemen.
Recognition: Long fuselage with small, upright rectangular air intakes. Long, tapered nose and small, rearward-hinged cockpit canopy; the lengthy dorsal tailfin extension is prominent. Variable-geometry wings, of wide span, have a drooping appearance when fully spread.
Variants: Initial full service production air superiority version (but with ground attack capability) was the MiG-23M 'Flogger-B', from which the MiG-23MF for export was developed. The lighter and more powerful MiG-23ML 'Flogger-G', with better radar and wider weapon compatibility, led to the MiG-23MLD 'Flogger-K' which incorporated various refinements. The

main ground attack variants of the type are the MiG-23BN 'Flogger-F' and the subsequent MiG-23BK/BM 'Flogger-H'. Two-seaters are named MiG-23UB 'Flogger-C'. The MiG-27 is an upgraded attack version, with increased weapon capabilities which was first developed as the 'Flogger-D' and then, with detail differences, the 'Flogger-J'.

Right: **The Czech Air Force operates this variable-geometry MiG-23 'Flogger' strike/fighter aircraft.** *PRM*

Mikoyan MiG-29 'Fulcrum'

Twin-turbofan single-seat fighter/attack aircraft
Basic data for MiG-29M
Powerplant: Two Klimov/Sariskov R-33K turbofans of 19,400lb st (86.3kN) with afterburner
Span: 37ft 3in (11.36m)
Length: 57ft 0in (17.37m)
Max speed: 1,518mph (2,445km/h)
Armament: One 30mm GSh-30-1 single-barrel cannon. Maximum external ordnance load of 9,920lb (4,500kg) on six underwing hardpoints — weaponry includes R-60MK (AA-8), R-27R1 (AA-10A), R-73E (AA-11) and R-77 (AA-12) AAMs; a variety of ASMs, namely the laser-guided Kh-25ML (AS-10) and Kh-29L (AS-14), the radar-homing Kh-31P/A (AS-17), and TV-guided Kh-29T (AS-14); plus bombs, including TV-guided stores, and rockets.
First aircraft flown: 6 October 1977
Entered service: August 1983
Current service: With the Russian armed forces; also in Bulgaria, Cuba, Germany, Hungary, India, Iran, Kazakhstan, Malaysia, North Korea, Peru, Poland, Romania, Slovakia, Syria, Ukraine and Yemen, plus with the USAF.

Below: **First flown on 6 October 1977 the MiG-29 'Fulcrum' has been exported to 17 countries.** *PRM*

Recognition: A long nose with a raised canopy. Broad-chord wings with highly swept leading-edges, swept leading-edge strokes blending into the forward fuselage. Underslung wedge-shaped engine air intakes either side of the fuselage. Widely-spaced twin fins, with pointed tips, with a small fillet extending along top of the wing fairing.

Variants: MiG-29A 'Fulcrum-A' is the original single-seat version; the MiG-29UB 'Fulcrum-B' is a two-seat operational trainer — it is these which serve with most of the type's overseas customers. The 'Fulcrum-C' development, the primary version in Russian service, has a more heavily-curved fuselage top decking, and provided the basis for the improved MiG-29S and the export MiG-29SE which continue to be offered by MIG-MAPO. A naval version, the carrier-capable MiG-29K, is also available but has not been ordered for production; the same is true of the MiG-29M, which is lighter, has all-new avionics and greater fuel capacity.

Mil Mi-8/17 'Hip'

Twin-turbine multi-purpose helicopter
Basic data for Mi-8T 'Hip-C'
Powerplant: Two Klimov TV2-117A turboshafts of 1,481eshp (1,104kW)
Rotor diameter: 69ft 10½in (21.29m)
Fuselage length: 59ft 7in (18.17m)
Max speed: 155mph (250km/h)
Armament: Most variants fitted with outriggers either side of the fuselage with two hardpoints for rockets in packs, or anti-tank missiles. Some have a flexibly-mounted 12.7mm machine gun in nose.
Accommodation: Two pilots and loadmaster. Main cabin can accommodate 28 troops, or 12 stretchers.
First aircraft flown: 24 June 1961 (Mi-8); 1976 (Mi-17)
Entered service: 1965 (Mi-8); 1977 (Mi-17)
Current service: Over 6,500 Mi-8s have been produced and production continues. Some 1,500 have been exported to around 60 countries.
Recognition: Mi-8 has the three-blade tail rotor on the starboard side of the fin, whereas that of the Mi-17 is on the port side. Conventional pod and boom configuration. Five-blade main rotor, inclined slightly forward. Horizontal stabiliser near end of tailboom. Tail rotor pylon forms small vertical stabiliser. Clamshell rear-loading freight doors. Non-retractable tricycle-type landing gear. Single wheel on main units and twin wheels on nose strut. Twin engines, with round nose cones, mounted close together above cabin. Large glazed area to nose.

Military versions have round windows on fuselage sides. Outriggers are braced from above. Weather radar in the nose for some versions.
Variants: Initial production Mi-8s, including the Mi-8T, are covered by the NATO designation 'Hip-C' and include the basic military transport plus civil versions with square windows; Mi-8TB 'Hip-E' is a dedicated assault version with three outrigger hardpoints. The Mi-14PS 'Haze-C' is a search and rescue version; Mi-14PL 'Haze-A' an ASW helicopter. Mi-8PS 'Hip-D' and Mi-8SMV 'Hip-J' are special missions versions. The Mi-17 'Hip-H' introduced uprated turboshafts and port side tail rotor; Mi-171 and Mi-172 have even more powerful engines.

Below: **Search and rescue is one of the varied uses of the Mil Mi-17 'Hip'.** *PRM*

Mil Mi-24/25/35 'Hind'

Assault and anti-armour helicopter
Basic data for Mi-24D 'Hind-D'
Powerplant: Two Klimov Tv3-117 turboshafts of 2,200eshp (1,633kW)
Rotor diameter: 56ft 9¼in (17.30m)
Fuselage length: 57ft 5¼in (17.51m)
Max speed: 208mph (335km/h)
Armament: 'Hind-D' has a 12.7mm four-barrel JakB rotary gun in a nose barbette and up to 3,300lb (1,500kg) of external ordnance; two anti-armour missiles may be carried on each stub wing endplate, and there are four underwing hardpoints for rockets and guns. 'Hind-E' has provision for 12 AT-6 Spiral anti-tank missiles, and the 'Hind-F' has a fixed twin-barrel 30mm cannon.
Accommodation: Crew of two, plus eight seats in cabin.
First aircraft flown: 19 September 1969
Entered service: 1973
Current service: Operates with the Russian armed forces; also in Afghanistan, Algeria, Angola, Armenia, Azerbaijan, Belarus, Bulgaria, Croatia, Cuba, Czech Republic, Georgia, Hungary, India, Iraq, Libya, Mozambique, Papua New Guinea, Peru, Poland, Slovakia, South Yemen, Syria, Ukraine, Vietnam and Yemen.
Recognition: Long narrow fuselage with stub wings carried high on the fuselage. Engines mounted above the cabin with a five-blade main rotor. Three-blade tail rotor on port side of tail boom with small pointed tailplane. Prominent chin radome. Fully retractable undercarriage.
Variants: Early Mi-24s, either 'Hind-A', 'B' or 'C', had a three-man crew under an extensive glasshouse canopy. This was replaced by separate tandem armoured-glass canopies in a steel-plated forward fuselage on subsequent aircraft, starting with the Mi-24D 'Hind-D' which was followed into service by the Mi-24V 'Hind-E'. A derivative of the 'Hind-D' is the Mi-24DU trainer with a faired-over gun turret. For export outside the Warsaw Pact states, the Mi-24D was known by Mil as the Mi-25, while the Mi-24V became the Mi-35 with better high-altitude engine performance. Other versions include the Mi-24P 'Hind-F', with a more powerful 30mm cannon, and two Russian reconnaissance variants, the Mi-24Rch and Mi-24K (both known as 'Hind-G').

Below: **This Mil Mi-24 V1 'Hind' of the Czech Air Force shows the armament carried by this attack helicopter.** *APM*

Mil Mi-26 'Halo'

Twin-turboshaft military and commercial heavy-lift helicopter
Basic data for Mi-26 'Halo-A'
Powerplant: Two ZKMB Progress D-136 turboshafts of 10,000eshp (7,460kW)
Rotor diameter: 105ft (32.00m)
Length: 110ft 8in (33.73m)
Max speed: 183mph (295km/h)
Accommodation: Crew of five, plus up to 80 fully equipped troops, 60 stretcher patients, or 44,000lb (20,000kg) internally
First aircraft flown: 14 December 1977
Entered service: 1983
Current service: With the Russian armed forces and India.
Recognition: Conventionally shaped helicopter with an eight-blade main rotor but with a fuselage of similar size to a C-130 Hercules with large rear clamshell doors. Engines are mounted above fuselage. A five-blade tail rotor on starboard side of swept fin. Small tailplane. Fixed undercarriage.
Variants: Mi-26 'Halo-A' is the basic military transport/assault helicopter, the

Mi-26T being a civil version. A flying crane variant with a glazed gondola, the Mi-26TM, and the Mi-26TP firefighter are also offered, along with the Mi-26TZ which is an airborne tanker for ground vehicles in inaccessible areas. The Mi-27 is an airborne command post development.

Below: **Mil Mi-26 'Halo' currently in service as a heavy-lift helicopter with the Russian Air Force.** *PRM*

Northrop F-5/T-38

Twin-turbojet single-seat light fighter/trainer
Basic data for F-5E Tiger II
Powerplant: Two General Electric J85-GE-21B turbojets of 3,000lb st (15.5kN) dry and 5,000lb st (22.4kN) with afterburner
Span: 26ft 8in (8.13m)
Length: 48ft 2in (14.68m)
Max speed: 1,082mph (1,742km/h)
Armament: Two 20mm M39A2 cannon, two AIM-9 Sidewinder missiles and up to 7,000lb (3,195kg) ordnance
First aircraft flown: 31 July 1963 (YF-5A); 11 August 1972 (F-5E)
Entered service: 30 April 1964 (F-5A); 4 April 1973 (F-5E)
Current service: With many air arms including Bahrain, Brazil, Canada, Iran, Indonesia, Jordan, Kenya, Malaysia, Mexico, Morocco, Norway, Paraguay, Saudi Arabia, Singapore, South Korea, Spain, Sudan, Switzerland, Taiwan, Thailand,

Tunisia, Turkey, Venezuela, Vietnam; also the USAF and USN.
Recognition: Long slender fuselage with an extended pointed nose. Angular fin and rudder linked to the prominent clearview cockpit canopy by a dorsal spine. Short-span low-set wings, swept on the leading-edge, with tip-tanks. Engine intakes above the wing roots. Tailplane set at the bottom of the rear fuselage with the twin jetpipes

Below: **Though the Northrop F-5 first flew in 1963 it is still in service with many air arms around the world.** *PRM*

extending beyond the tail.

Variants: The initial T-38 Talon was purchased in quantity by the USAF, and remains in service. The F-5A single-seat, F-5B two-seat and RF-5A reconnaissance fighters were supplied to overseas air arms as the Freedom Fighter. The longer, heavier, improved-handling NF-5A/5B was produced in the Netherlands (surplus aircraft having been sold to Turkey). The F-5E Tiger II and two-seat F-5F are in service with the USAF and USN as tactical aggressor trainers. Bristol Aerospace in Canada has modified CF-5A/Bs as CF-116 lead-in trainers for the CF-18. F-5 retrofit programmes to include new avionics and other updated systems are being widely undertaken, notably for Norway's F-5A/Bs (the Sierra Industries Tiger PAWS programme) and Chile's F-5E/Fs (an IAI/ENAER upgrade).

Northrop Grumman B-2 Spirit

Low-observable strategic penetration bomber

Basic data for B-2A

Powerplant: Four General Electric F118-GE-110 non-afterburning turbofans of 19,000lb st (84.kN)

Span: 172ft 0in (52.43m)

Length: 69ft 0in (21.03m)

Max speed: Mach 0.8

Armament: Boeing rotary launcher assembly (RLA) in each of two side-by-side weapons bays in lower centre-body. Total capacity of 16 AGM-131 SRAM II or AGM-129 ACMs or 16 AGM-137 TSSAMs. Alternative weapons include 16 B61 tactical/strategic or 80 x 500lb Mk 82 bombs, 80 Mk 62 aerial mines, plus enhanced GBU-30 capability. No external pylons.

Crew: Two, with provision for third member

First aircraft flown: 17 July 1989

Entered service: 17 December 1993

Current service: With the USAF

Recognition: Blended flying-wing, with straight leading-edges, swept at 33°. 'Double-W' trailing-edge incorporating elevons and drag rudders outboard of engines, which are mounted in pairs within wing structure. Engines fed by S-shaped ducts. Two auxiliary air inlet doors mounted on top of intake trunks remain closed on ground and in low-speed flight. Two V-shaped overwing exhausts set well forward of trailing-edge. Two large dielectric panels on the undersurface, each side of the nose, cover the radar antenna. Inward-retracting four-wheel main bogies and rearward-retracting two-wheel nose unit. Four flightdeck windows.

Variants: Different block number aircraft have incorporated various modifications, the latest being Block 30 (new-build aircraft and upgrades).

Below: **The B-2A Spirit flying wing strategic bomber first entered service with the USAF in December 1993.** *PRM*

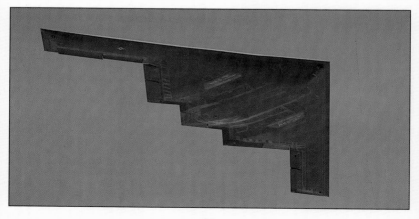

Northrop Grumman E-2 Hawkeye

Twin-turboprop carrier-borne airborne early warning/command and control (AEW/CC) aircraft

Basic data for E-2C Hawkeye II
Powerplant: Two Allison T56-A-427 turboprops of 5,100eshp (3,803kW)
Span: 80ft 7in (24.56m)
Length: 57ft 7in (17.55m)
Max speed: 383mph (617km/h)
Crew: Five (two pilots and three systems operators)
First aircraft flown: 21 October 1960 (E-2A); 20 January 1971 (E-2C)
Entered service: 19 January 1964 (E-2A); November 1973 (E-2C)
Current service: With the US Navy, Egypt, France, Japan, Singapore and Taiwan.
Recognition: Long oval-section fuselage. High-set unswept wings with the engines extending well forward and below. A large circular radome is mounted on four struts above the rear fuselage. There are two large vertical fins at the ends of the dihedralled tailplane with two smaller fins inboard.
Variants: The original model was the E-2A, subsequently modified to the E-2B with improved systems. A totally revised electronic system and surveillance radar was installed in the E-2C which has progressively been updated to the APS139 standard. Northrop Grumman is contracted to build mission computer upgrades (MCUs) for new-build aircraft, such as those which are to be supplied to the French Navy. The TE-2C is a US Navy training variant.

Below: **The Northrop Grumman E-2C Hawkeye is the US Navy's airborne early warning aircraft.** *PRM*

Panavia Tornado IDS/GR1

Above: **For maritime strike the RAF operates the GR1B version of the Panavia Tornado.** *PRM*

Twin-turbofan two-seat multi-role strike and electronic reconnaissance aircraft
Basic data for IDS/GR1
Powerplant: Two Turbo Union RB199-103 turbofans of 8,650lb st (38.5kN) dry and 16,075lb st (71.5kN) with afterburner
Span: 45ft 7¼in (13.90m) wings spread
Length: 54ft 9½in (16.70m)
Max speed: 1,452mph (2,336km/h)
Armament: IDS/GR1 in various variants has two 27mm IWKA-Mauser cannon, and can carry up to 19,840lb of ordnance including the BAe ALARM anti-radiation missile, bombs including the laser-guided Paveway II, the JP233 airfield denial weapon, BAe Sea Eagle anti-ship weapon, plus AIM-9s for self defence on RAF aircraft; German AF machines can be equipped with AGM-65 and AGM-88 HARM, as can Italian aircraft; the German Navy uses the MBB Kormoran anti-ship missile.
First aircraft flown: 14 August 1974
Entered service: July 1980
Current service: With the RAF, Italian AF,

German Navy and AF, Royal Saudi AF.
Recognition: Short, broad fuselage with a very large swept fin and rudder. Shoulder-mounted variable geometry wings of delta shape when fully swept. Bubble two-seat tandem cockpit and a short nose cone. All-moving tailplane on the sides of the twin tailpipes.
Variants: Tornado IDS (GR1 in RAF service) was developed for the RAF, German AF and Navy, and Italian AF. Each service has a small number of combat-capable dual-control aircraft for operational/conversion training. All these basic strike versions are being updated — the RAF aircraft becoming GR4s with new avionics and TIALD capability, while Germany and Italy are jointly carrying out mid-life improvements. In the reconnaissance role, the RAF operates the GR1A, while the German and Italian AFs use the ECR (able to carry the AGM-88 HARM). Sea Eagle-armed GR1Bs equip two RAF squadrons for maritime strike duties.

Panavia Tornado ADV/F3

Above: Three air arms operate the two-seat, all-weather Panavia Tornado F3. *PRM*

Twin-turbofan two-seat all-weather fighter

Basic data for Tornado F3

Powerplant: Two Turbo Union RB199-104 turbofans of 9,100lb st (40.48kN) dry and 16,520lb st (73.48kN) with afterburner

Span: 45ft 7½in (13.91m) wings spread

Length: 61ft 3½in (18.68m)

Max speed: 1,453mph (2,338km/h)

Armament: Four each of BAe Sky Flash and AIM-9L Sidewinder AAMs; only one 27mm IWKA-Mauser cannon, on the port side

First aircraft flown: 27 October 1979 (ADV prototype); 20 November 1985 (F3)

Entered service: 1984 (F2); 28 July 1986 (F3)

Current service: With the RAF, Italian AF and Royal Saudi AF.

Recognition: Basically retains most of the main features of the IDS/GR1, but is 4ft 6in (1.37m) longer. The resulting extension of the nose makes for a more 'gentle', less stubby profile.

Variants: The RAF's Tornado F3s, of which production ceased in 1993, are basically the same as the Saudi ADVs. In 1995, the Italian AF received the first of a batch of F3s leased from the RAF as a stopgap measure before the arrival of EF2000 — these can be armed with the Selenia Aspide AAM, but have otherwise not been modified.

Pilatus PC-7 Turbo Trainer

Single-engined two-seat light turboprop trainer

Basic data for PC-7

Powerplant: One Pratt & Whitney PT6A-25A turboprop of 560eshp (417.6kW)

Span: 34ft 1½in (10.40m)

Length: 32ft 0in (9.75m)

Max speed: 256mph (412km/h)

Armament: Underwing hardpoints for up to 2,293lb (1,040kg) of ordnance

First aircraft flown: 12 April 1966 (P-3B); 12 May 1975 (PC-7)

Entered service: 1979 (PC-7)

Current service: With Switzerland, plus Angola, Austria, Bolivia, Chad, Chile, France, Guatemala, Iran, Iraq, Malaysia, Mexico, Myanmar, Netherlands, South Africa, Surinam and UAE.

Recognition: Slender fuselage with a clear 'glasshouse' tandem cockpit canopy at midpoint. Low-set constant-chord wings below the cockpit. Tall fin and rudder, square topped, with a dorsal fillet. Wide tailplane set at the base of the rudder.

Variants: The original Pilatus P-3B was a turboprop derivative of the P-3 piston-engined trainer. It was not developed into its present configuration until 1975; the production turboprop PC-7 was first flown in August 1978 and has subsequently received substantial orders, including of course from the Swiss AF. The PC-7 Mk II (developed to meet the South African AF's requirement for a Harvard replacement) incorporates a stepped cockpit, improved aerodynamics and a more powerful PT6A-25C engine of 700shp (522kW).

Below: **Widely used as a pilot trainer, the Pilatus PC-7 has been in service since 1979.** *PRM*

Pilatus PC-9/Raytheon Beech T-6 Texan II

Single-turboprop two-seat trainer
Basic data for PC-9
Powerplant: One Pratt & Whitney PT6A-62 turboprop of 950eshp (708.4kW)
Span: 33ft 3in (10.12m)
Length: 33ft 5in (10.18m)
Max speed: 345mph (556km/h)
Armament: Can carry underwing stores
First aircraft flown: 7 May 1984
Entered service: 1987
Current service: Soon to enter USAF and USN service as the T-6; also used by the Swiss AF, and the air arms of Australia, Croatia, Cyprus, Myanmar, Saudi Arabia, Slovenia and Thailand. Civilian-operated PC-9s support the German AF as target tugs.

Recognition: The PC-9/T-6A is similar in some respects to the PC-7, but there are numerous recognition differences — it is a taller aircraft than its predecessor, with a longer, more sloping nose and four-blade propeller. It has a pronounced, stepped cockpit configuration with an extensive glass area, giving a 'hump-backed' appearance, and is equipped with a ventral airbrake.

Variants: The standard PC-9 trainer, as operated by Australia (built locally) has been developed into a target tug — the Swiss AF aircraft are all configured thus, as are the civilian-operated PC-9Bs which support the German AF. Latest development is the Mk II, which was selected to meet the USAF/USN JPATS (Joint Primary Aircraft Training System) requirement, and up to 711 examples will be produced by Raytheon Beech as the T-6A Texan II. This aircraft, capable of training at day or night, has a PT6A-68 engine of 1,250eshp (932.1kW), improved avionics and is pressurised.

Left: **The Raytheon Beech T-6A Texan II was the winner of the USAF/USN JPATS competition.** *PRM*

Pilatus Britten-Norman BN-2 Defender/Islander

Twin-piston/turboprop utility transport
Basic data for BN-2T Turbine Islander
Powerplant: Two Allison 250-B17C turboprops of 400eshp (298kW)
Span: 49ft 0in (14.94m); 53ft 0in (16.15m) with extended wingtips
Length: 35ft 7¾in (10.86m)
Max speed: 212mph (341km/h)
Armament: Defender can have four underwing hardpoints for rocket pods, machine guns, bombs, missiles or fuel tanks.
Accommodation: One crew and nine passengers (BN-2T)
First aircraft flown: 13 June 1965 (BN-2A); 2 August 1980 (BN-2T)
Entered service: November 1971 (BN-2B Defender)
Current service: With the RAF and Army Air Corps, and air arms in Belgium, Belize, Botswana, Democratic Republic of Congo, Eire, Guyana, India, Indonesia, Jamaica, Malawi, Mexico, Panama, Philippines, Seychelles, Surinam, Turkey, UAE, Venezuela and Zimbabwe.

Recognition: Engines mounted below and forward of the straight, high-set 'plank' wing. Fixed tricycle undercarriage, with the mainwheels on an extended, faired leg at the rear of the engines, and the nosewheel situated well forward below the nose cone. Slab-sided rectangular fuselage with a level top surface and gently-raked lower surface aft of the wing. Two port-side cabin entry doors and large rectangular cabin windows. The tall, angular fin and rudder have a small dorsal fillet; the straight tailplane is mounted on top of the fuselage, below the rudder. The extended wingtips on some aircraft have a distinctive conical camber.

Variants: The BN-2, BN-2A and BN-2B are all

Above: A Pilatus Britten-Norman Islander AL1 operated by the Army Air Corps. *DJM*

broadly similar piston-engined versions. The latter two variants can be equipped with additions which include a lengthened nose and/or 4ft 0in (1.22m) extended wingtips. The BN-2T has Allison 250 turboprops in place of the Lycoming series piston engines, and it is this version in Defender form which is used by the AAC. Various specialist configurations include airborne early warning, maritime patrol and battlefield surveillance with nose radar. Numerous AEW Defenders have been marketed including the MSSA (Multi-Sensor Surveillance Aircraft) fitted with APG-66 radar in a bulbous radome, together with FLIR and GPS. The Defender 4000 maritime patroller (recently sold to the Irish Garda, operated by the Irish Air Corps) features the Trislander's wing.

Rockwell B-1 Lancer

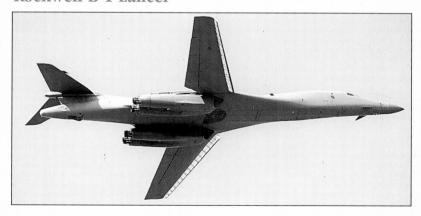

Above: The Rockwell B-1B is in service with the USAF as a long-range conventional and nuclear bomber. *PRM*

Four-turbofan variable-geometry strategic bomber

Basic data for B-1B

Powerplant: Four General Electric F101-GE-102 turbofans of 14,600lb st (64.9kN) dry and 30,780lb st (136.9kN) with afterburner

Span: 136ft 8½in (41.67m) wings spread

Length: 147ft 0in (44.81m)

Max speed: 822mph (1,325km/h)

Armament: Up to 28,000lb (12,701kg) externally and 75,000lb (34,020kg) internally, including AGM-86B cruise missiles, B-611/B-83 nuclear bombs, AGM-69A short-range attack missiles or various conventional bomb/missile loads.

Crew: Four

First aircraft flown: 23 December 1974 (B-1A); 18 October 1984 (B-1B)

Entered service: 27 July 1985 (B-1B)

Current service: With the USAF only.

Recognition: Long sleek fuselage with a small swept fin and mid-mounted tailplane. The low-set variable-geometry wings have a relatively narrow chord when spread. The four turbofans are slung under the fuselage/wing centre-section. The flightdeck is moulded into the pointed nose and forward fuselage to give a humped appearance.

Variants: The B-1B is the operational version of the original B-1A development aircraft. The final aircraft, of a production run of 100, was delivered on 30 April 1988.

Saab 35 Draken

Single-turbojet single-seat all-weather fighter/two-seat trainer

Basic data for J35J

Powerplant: One Volvo Flygmotor RM6C turbojet of 12,790lb st (56.89kN) dry and 17,650lb st (78.51kN) with afterburner.

Span: 30ft 10in (9.40m)

Length: 50ft 4in (15.35m)

Max speed: 1,320mph (2,125km/h)

Armament: Two 30mm Aden cannon and four Rb24 Sidewinder or Rb27 Falcon AAMs, plus up to 9,900lb (4,500kg) of ordnance.

First aircraft flown: 25 October 1955

Entered service: March 1960

Current service: With the Austrian, Finnish and Swedish air forces.

Recognition: A distinctive double-delta wing with the engine intakes at the forward wing roots. The second delta is less sharply angled. A large fin, well swept on the forward edge, with the reheat jetpipe extending behind it. The single-

place cockpit canopy is forward of the intakes and overlooks the short pointed nose which has a pitot tube extending from it.

Variants: The initial J35A was replaced by the J35B with better armament; these were subsequently modified to the J35D with a more powerful engine and improved autopilot. A two-seat trainer (Sk35) was also produced, along with the S35E reconnaissance variant. The J35F was equipped with Falcon missiles and a single Aden cannon. Updated J35J (now the primary Swedish AF operational version), based on the J35F has modified radar, improved infra-red sensor and two additional stores pylons fitted for additional weapons or auxiliary fuel tanks. Austria flies the J35Ö, operated with podded reconnaissance equipment.

Below: **A long-serving Swedish Air Force Saab J35J Draken.** *PRM*

Saab 37 Viggen

Single-turbofan single-seat multi-role fighter/two-seat trainer
Basic data for JA37

Powerplant: One Volvo Flygmotor RM8B turbofan of 16,203lb st (72.1kN) dry and 28,108lb st (125kN) with afterburner

Span: 34ft 9¼in (10.60m)

Length: 51ft 2in (15.58m)

Max speed: 1,320mph (2,125km/h)

Armament: The various versions produced can carry up to 15,432lb (7,000kg) ordnance under wings and fuselage including 30mm Oerlikon KCA cannon, Rb27/8 Falcon, Rb74 Sidewinder, Rb71 Skyflash, Rb15F anti-ship and Rb75 Maverick missiles, rockets and bombs.

First aircraft flown: 8 February 1967 (AJ37); 27 September 1974 (JA37)

Entered service: June 1971 (AJ37); 1978 (JA37)

Current service: With the Swedish AF

Recognition: Two separate delta wings — a small foreplane (canard) just aft of the cockpit above the fuselage engine intakes and a much larger main delta wing extending to the tailpipe along the bottom of the fuselage. The tailfin is large and triangular with a small cone at the base of the rudder above the jetpipe. The cockpit is relatively small and merges into a spine which extends to the tail. The conical nose comes to a point with a short pitot tube. Tandem mainwheels retract into the rear delta wing.

Variants: Viggens are designated according to their principal role, with appropriate armament and equipment: AJ37 — all-weather attack; JA37 — all-weather interceptor; SF37 — reconnaissance fighter; SH37 — maritime reconnaissance fighter; and Sk37 — two-seat combat trainer. Production ended with the 149th aircraft, delivered 29 June 1990, but around 62 Viggens of the AJ, SF and SH derivatives are being upgraded to multi-role AJS37 standard with an expanded range of weaponry available for carriage, and new avionics.

Below: **The unusual double-delta Saab JA37 Viggen flown by the Swedish Air Force.** *PRM*

Saab JAS 39 Gripen

Single-seat all-weather, all-altitude interceptor, attack and reconnaissance aircraft

Basic data for JAS 39A

Powerplant: One General Electric/Volvo Flygmotor RM12 (F404-GE-400) turbofan of 12,140lb st (54.06kN) with afterburner

Span: 27ft 6¾in (8.40m)

Length: 46ft 3in (14.10m)

Max speed: 1,321mph (2,126km/h)

Armament: One fixed 27mm Mauser Bk27 cannon, internally mounted. Wingtip stations for RB674 (AIM-9) AAMs. One centreline and four underwing hardpoints for rockets, DWS39 cluster bomb dispensers, RB675 (AGM-65) ASMs, RBS15 anti-ship missiles, bombs, AIM-120 or Matra Mica AAMs.

First aircraft flown: 9 December 1988 (JAS 39A); 29 April 1996 (JAS 39B)

Entered service: 8 June 1993 (JAS 39A)

Current service: With the Swedish AF

Recognition: Delta wing, with squared tips for missile rails, having 45° leading-edge sweepback. Independently moveable foreplanes (canards) with leading-edge sweep of 43°. Dog-tooth wing leading-edge and two elevon surfaces at each trailing-edge. Single mainwheels retract forward into fuselage and twin nosewheel retracts rearward. Near rectangular engine intakes on either side of fuselage, each with splitter plate, ahead of foreplanes. Prominent exhaust cone at rear of fuselage. Long pointed nose. Swept leading-edge to large fin, which has square tip. Three projections to leading-edge of fin.

Variants: JAS 39A — standard single-seater; JAS 39B — two-seater (Gripen SK) with fuselage plug and lengthened cockpit canopy, no internal gun; JAS 39C and D — potential improved Swedish versions of A and B with enhanced data handling capability; JAS 39X — potential export version, to be upgraded to standard of C/D.

Below: Saab JAS39 Gripens entered service with the Swedish Air Force in June 1993. *PRM*

Saab 105

Twin-turbojet two-seat light attack/trainer

Basic data for Saab 105ÖE

Powerplant: Two General Electric J85-GE-17B turbojets of 2,850lb st (12.96kN)

Span: 31ft 2in (9.50m)

Length: 34ft 5in (10.50m)

Max speed: 603mph (970km/h)

Armament: Six underwing hardpoints for up to 4,410lb (2,000kg) of ordnance

First aircraft flown: 29 June 1963 (Sk60); 29 April 1967 (105XT)

Entered service: March 1966

Current service: With the Swedish and Austrian air forces

Recognition: Short tapered fuselage with an angular 'T' tail. The slightly-swept wings are mounted on top of the fuselage and are anhedralled. A large bubble cockpit canopy is situated forward of the wings and overlooks a long conical nose. The engine intakes are on the fuselage sides below the wings.

Variants: The Sk60A was a basic trainer for the Swedish AF, a number being modified to Sk60Bs with an attack capability. The Sk60C, first flown in 1967, was a reconnaissance/attack/trainer with an extended nose. An export development, the 105XT, was purchased by Austria designated 105ÖE; it had GE J85 turbojets in place of the original Turboméca Aubisques, which gave it increased performance and weapon load. Sweden's Sk60 fleet is being re-engined with Williams Rolls FJ44 turbofans, the first prototype making its maiden flight in October 1995.

Below: **Saab 105s are only in service with the Swedish and Austrian Air Forces.** *PRM*

Saab MFI-17 Supporter

Single piston-engined light trainer and multi-role tactical aircraft
Basic data for T-17 Supporter

Powerplant: One Avco Lycoming IO-360-A1B6 piston engine of 200hp (150kW)

Span: 29ft 0in (8.85m)

Length: 22ft 11½in (7.00m)

Max speed: 146mph (236km/h)

Armament: Six underwing hardpoints can be fitted to the basic aircraft for up to 1,480lb (673kg) of stores including gun packs, Bofors Bantam anti-tank missiles and supply packs.

Accommodation: Two side-by-side seats for instructor and student

First aircraft flown: 6 July 1972

Entered service: October 1974

Current service: In Denmark and Zambia

Recognition: Distinctive angular appearance with broad-chord high-set braced wings slightly swept forward. Two-place cockpit forward of the wing with a clearview canopy extending above the wing. Swept fin and rudder with a squared-off top; the high-set tailplane is rectangular in shape. A fixed tricycle undercarriage.

Variants: The Supporter was developed from the MFI-15 Safari. The Royal Danish AF variant is known as the T-17, and the type was also produced in Pakistan by PAC and named Mushshak (Proficient).

Right: **Saab's T-17 Supporter, sold as a trainer and light observation aircraft to the Royal Danish AF.** *APM*

SEPECAT Jaguar

Twin-turbofan tactical support/fighter aircraft
Basic data for Jaguar A/GR1A
Powerplant: Two Turboméca/Rolls-Royce Adour 104 turbofans of 5,320lb st (23.7kN)
Span: 28ft 6in (8.69m)
Length: 55ft 2½in (16.83m) including probe
Max speed: 1,005mph (1,700km/h)
Armament: Two 30mm Aden cannon, and up to 10,000lb (4,500kg) of stores — RAF aircraft can carry bombs including Paveway II LGBs and cluster bombs, rockets, and AIM-9 Sidewinders mounted on overwing rails. French Jaguars may also be equipped with laser-guided and cluster bombs, together with Martel anti-radar missiles and Matra Magic AAMs.
First aircraft flown: 8 September 1968
Entered service: With the French AF in 1973 and RAF in 1974
Current service: RAF and French AF, and the air arms of Ecuador, India, Nigeria and Oman.
Recognition: Long sleek fuselage with a large swept tailfin and rudder. Relatively short-span swept wings are shoulder-mounted on the fuselage. The internal jet engines have intakes either side of the fuselage behind the cockpit,

with their top surfaces forming an extension of the wing. The rear jetpipes are located forward and below the tailplane which has marked anhedral. The raised bubble canopy is set above the sharply-pointed nose. The twin mainwheels of the undercarriage retract into the fuselage.
Variants: The RAF primarily operates the GR1A single-seat and T2A two-seat derivatives, now augmented by the GR1B and corresponding T2B which are equipped with TIALD pods. In French service, single- and two-seat aircraft are designated Jaguar A and E respectively. The trainer variants have an extended front fuselage with a two-place tandem cockpit. For export, the Jaguar International (also licence-built by HAL in India as the Shamsher, meaning 'assault sword') features uprated Adour Mk 811 turbofans (of 8,400lb st) and improved avionics. An upgrade for RAF Jaguars will result in the GR3 version, capable of carrying ASRAAMs and with numerous other weapon and avionics enhancements.

Below: **The SEPECAT Jaguar continues in the ground-attack/reconnaissance role with the RAF.** *PRM*

Shorts Tucano

Single-turboprop two-seat basic military trainer.
Basic data for Tucano T1
Powerplant: One Garrett TPE331-12-B turboprop of 1,100eshp (820kW)
Span: 37ft 0in (11.28m)
Length: 32ft 4in (9.86m)
Max speed: 322mph (519km/h)

Armament: Kuwaiti and Kenyan aircraft can be armed with machine gun pods, rockets and up to 551lb (250kg) of bombs
First aircraft flown: 16 August 1980 (EMB312 Tucano); 30 December 1986 (Shorts)
Entered service: 16 June l988 (T1)
Current service: With the RAF, Kenya and Kuwait
Recognition: Low-set unswept wings without tip

tanks. Rudder extends beyond the trailing-edge of the tailplane. Large clearview canopy covering the tandem cockpit, with the rear seat higher than the front. Large exhausts on the forward cowling sides.

Variants: The Shorts-built Tucano T1, with the

more powerful engine, has nearly 1,000 changes making it 50% different from the original Embraer EMB312. Main difference is the adoption of the TPE331 engine. Kenya and Kuwait operate the Mk 51 and 52 versions, largely similar to the RAF T1s.

Left: **Shorts Tucano T1, in service with the RAF as a basic training aircraft.** *PRM*

SIAI-Marchetti SF260

Single-engined two-seat light trainer/support aircraft
Basic data for SF260W Warrior
Powerplant: One Lycoming O-540-E4A5 piston engine of 260hp (195kW)
Span: 27ft 4¾in (8.35m)
Length: 23ft 3½in (7.10m)
Max speed: 215mph (347km/h)
Armament: Up to 660lb (300kg) of ordnance on underwing pylons, including gun pods, bombs, practice bombs and rockets
First aircraft flown: 15 July 1964 (SF260); May 1972 (SF260W)
Entered service: 1973 (SF260W)
Current service: With the air arms of Belgium, Bolivia, Burma, Democratic Republic of Congo, Dubai, Ecuador, Eire, Italy, Libya, Morocco, Nicaragua, Philippines, Singapore, Sri Lanka, Thailand, Turkey, Tunisia, Zambia and Zimbabwe.
Recognition: Short fuselage with a tall fin and rudder. A dorsal extension reaches the rear of the large bubble cockpit canopy. The low-set wings are unswept with medium chord; wingtip fuel tanks are standard.
Variants: The initial civil versions were the SF260A, B and C. The unarmed SF260M military trainer was first flown in October

1970. Strengthened fuselage and wings were needed for the SF260W Warrior to enable the carriage of underwing stores. This variant was flown in May 1972 and was followed by the SF260SW Sea Warrior, equipped with wingtip radar and reconnaissance pods. The SF260TP is powered by an Allison 250-B17D turboprop of 350eshp (260kW), maximum speed being increased to 264mph (425km/h).

Below: **A SIAI-Marchetti SF260 pilot trainer of the Belgian Air Force.** *APM*

Sikorsky S-61/Westland Sea King

Multi-purpose medium-lift ASW, SAR and assault helicopter
Basic data for Sea King HAS6
Powerplant: Two Rolls-Royce H1400-1T Gnome turboshafts of 1,660eshp (1,240kW)
Rotor diameter: 62ft 0in (18.90m)
Length: 55ft 9¾in (17.01m)
Max speed: 143mph (230km/h)
Armament: Four Mk 44 torpedoes, two Mk 46 torpedoes or 850lb depth charges can be carried; door-mounted machine guns can be fitted, and also sponsons for rockets.
Accommodation: Crew of two, and 28 troops
First aircraft flown: 11 March 1959 (S-61), 7 May 1969 (Sea King HAS1)
Entered service: 1970 (HAS1)
Current service: With the US Navy (SH-3), the RAF (HAR3/3A) and RN (HAS6, HC4 AEW2, HU5) and also in Argentina, Australia, Belgium, Brazil, Canada, Denmark, Egypt, Germany, India, Italy, Japan, Malaysia, Norway, Pakistan, Qatar, Spain and Thailand.
Recognition: Long fuselage with boat-hull bottom and sponsons either side of the cabin into which the main undercarriage wheels retract. Engines mounted above the cabin with the five-blade main rotor on top. Short tail section stepped up behind the single rear wheel. Six-blade tail rotor on port side of the short stabiliser. ASW Sea King versions have a large dustbin radar on top of the fuselage behind the engines.
Variants: The Sikorsky SH-3 has been gradually phased out of USN service, the SH-3H being the final development of the line in recent years with relatively few now remaining. It was additionally built by Agusta in Italy and Mitsubishi in Japan, while Canada's CH-124s were also assembled locally. Operators of the S-61 include Denmark, whose aircraft are used only for SAR work. Westland-built Sea Kings have been ordered in many forms, not least the RN — currently in service are the HAS6 for ASW duties, the airborne early warning AEW2 with Searchwater radar, the HC4 commando assault transport (with a fixed undercarriage) and the utility HU5. RAF operations of the Sea King are for SAR tasks, the HAR3 now augmented by the improved HAR3A. Overseas customers have ordered various different export marks, such as Belgium's Mk 48, Germany's Mk 41 and Norway's Mk 43. Export versions for troop-carrying are named Commando, such as those of Egypt and Qatar.

Below: Westland Sea Kings HAS5 in service with the Royal Navy. *PRM*

Sikorsky S-65/H-53

Two-/three-turboshaft heavy-lift utility helicopter

Basic data for CH-53E Super Stallion

Powerplant: Three General Electric T64-GE-416 turboshafts of 4,380eshp (3,265kW)

Rotor diameter: 79ft 0in (24.08m)

Length: 73ft 5in (22.38m)

Max speed: 196mph (315km/h)

Armament: MH-53Js can be equipped with three 7.62mm Miniguns in the side doors and rear ramp.

Accommodation: Crew of three and up to 55 troops; 30,000lb (13,636kg) payload

First aircraft flown: 14 October 1964 (CH-53A); 1 March 1974 (CH-53E)

Entered service: January 1967 (CH-53A); June 1981 (CH-53E)

Current service: With the USAF, Marine Corps and Navy; other operators are Germany, Iran, Israel and Japan.

Recognition: Very long cabin section with a short tail boom and stabilator. Seven-blade single main rotor mounted above the engines over the forward cabin. Rear ramp loading door for access to the cabin. Four-blade tail rotor on port side of fin and large braced tailplane on the starboard side. Fully retractable nosewheel undercarriage with the main wheels housed in fairings on the cabin sides. Additional long-range fuel tanks can be fitted to the fairings. Many of the current variants serving with the US forces are equipped with a refuelling probe.

Variants: Designed as the S-65 series, the original CH-53A for the USMC was the first of the line to see service (all now retired except for some sold to Israel). It gave rise to the more powerful CH-53D, and then numerous other derivatives — the CH-53G for the German Army, and Israeli S-65Cs remain much-used, while 39 USAF CH/HH-53s (the rest now phased out) have been converted to MH-53J Pave Low III Enhanced standard, with advanced avionics and many other enhancements. These, the most powerful helicopters in the US forces, support Special Operations forces 'behind enemy lines' and act as long-range combat rescue helicopters with a third tasking of civilian SAR. The S-80 series has spawned the three-engined CH-53E, the most numerous USN and USMC variant, along with the MH-53E Sea Dragon minesweeper.

Below: **Sikorsky MH-53J used for special duties by the USAF.** *PRM*

Sikorsky S-70/H-60 Black Hawk

Medium-lift assault/utility helicopter

Basic data for UH-60A

Powerplant: Two General Electric T700-GE-700 turboshafts of 1,560eshp (1,150kW)

Rotor diameter: 53ft 8in (16.23m)

Length: 50ft ¾in (15.26m)

Max speed: 184mph (296km/h)

Armament: Can carry pintle-mounted Miniguns or 7.62mm M60 machine guns; USAF HH-60Gs are similarly equipped, while MH-60Gs and USN HH-60Hs are fitted with 12.7mm machine guns

Accommodation: Three crew plus 11 troops or 8,000lb underslung

First aircraft flown: 17 October 1974 (YUH-60A); October 1978 (UH-60A)

Entered service: June 1979

Current service: With the USAF and US Army; also, in various versions, in Argentina, Australia, Bahrain, Brunei, China, Colombia, Egypt, Israel, Japan, Jordan, Malaysia, Mexico, Morocco, Philippines, Saudi Arabia, South Korea, Taiwan and Turkey.

Recognition: Streamlined fuselage with flat underside and curved top surface which incorporates the two engines above the cabin. Single four-blade main rotor. Fixed undercarriage with mainwheels at the front of the cabin and a single wheel halfway along the fuselage. Four-blade tail rotor on the starboard side of the vertical stabilator. Large tailplane below the rotor. Cabin doors with large rectangular windows slide to rear to give easy entry.

Variants: UH-60A produced for US Army in several versions — assault, utility and casevac, all convertible. There have been numerous other versions — the EH-60C for battlefield jamming, HH-60G and MH-60G Pave Hawk used by the USAF for combat rescue and Special Operations duties, and US Army Special Ops MH-60Ks. The latest US Army UH-60L has 20% more power from its T700-GE-701C engine. Export sales of the S-70A (equivalent to the UH-60A) have been considerable, including licence production in Australia and Japan.

Below: The US Army's Sikorsky UH-60 Black Hawk battlefield support helicopter. *PRM*

Sikorsky S-70/SH-60 Seahawk

Anti-submarine warfare and anti-ship surveillance and targeting helicopter
Basic data for SH-60B/S-70B
Powerplant: Two General Electric T700-GE-401C turboshafts of 1,800eshp (1,342kW)
Rotor diameter: 53ft 8in (16.36m)
Fuselage length: 50ft ⅜in (15.26m)
Max speed: 167mph (268km/h)
Armament: Bendix AQS-13F dipping sonar and Mk 46 and 50 torpedoes, AGM-119B Penguin anti-ship missiles, plus pintle-mounted machine guns or Hellfire anti-armour missiles. HH-60Fs can carry 7.62mm Miniguns, 12.7mm machine guns and rocket pods.
Crew: Three
First aircraft flown: 12 December 1979
Entered service: 1983
Current service: With the US Navy and Coast Guard, plus Australia, Greece, Japan, Spain, Taiwan and Thailand.
Recognition: Streamlined fuselage with flat underside and curved top surface which incorporates the two engines above the cabin. Single four-blade main rotor. Fixed undercarriage with main wheels at the front of the cabin and two twin-wheels on fuselage stubs under engines. Four-blade tail rotor on the starboard side of the vertical stabilizer. Large tailplane.

Variants: First to be produced for the US Navy was the SH-60B Seahawk, which is used as a LAMPS (Light Airborne Multi-Purpose System) helicopter primarily operating on ASW duties. The SH-60F Ocean Hawk, a further development, does not have the LAMPS function and flies on 'inner zone' ASW operations, providing close-in protection for USN carrier battle groups. Both these versions will be upgraded to a common SH-60R standard with dipping sonar and search radar. The HH-60H Rescue Hawk is the USN's primary combat rescue helicopter with various armament combinations. The Seahawk has been exported to various countries as the S-70B, licence-produced in Australia and Japan, while the US Coast Guard uses the HH-60J Jayhawk as a medium-range recovery helicopter. A hybrid of the UH-60L Black Hawk and SH-60F Seahawk is designated CH-60, for fleet combat support, and was first flown in October 1997.

Right: A Sikorsky SH-60 Seahawk of the US Navy. *APM*

Sukhoi Su-22 'Fitter'

Single-seat variable geometry ground attack fighter, reconnaissance aircraft and two-seat combat trainer
Basic data for Su-22M-4 'Fitter-K'
Powerplant: One Saturn/Lyulka AL-21F-3 turbojet of 17,200lb st (76.59kN), or 24,800lb (110.44kN) with afterburner
Span: 44ft 11in (13.68m) wings spread
Length: 52ft 1in (15.87m)
Max speed: 1,150mph (1,850km/h)
Armament: Two 30mm NR-30 guns, one in each wing root. Nine hardpoints for 8,820lb of

armament including bombs, gun pods, rockets, two R-13M, R-60 or R-73A AAMs; Kh-25ML, Kh-27, Kh-29 and Kh-58 ASMs. Four SPPU-22 gun pods can be fitted, with a downward attack capability.

First aircraft flown: 1977

Current service: With the Russian armed forces (including 120 for ground attack, 50 for reconnaissance with tactical air forces and 35 with Naval Aviation); also with the air forces of Afghanistan, Belarus, Czech Republic, Peru, Poland, Slovakia and Vietnam.

Recognition: Conventional mid-wing all-swept

monoplane with variable geometry outer wings (selected positions of 30°, 45° and 63°). Circular fuselage with slightly drooped nose. Ram intake with variable shock-cone centrebody. Pitot on port side of nose. Deep dorsal spine leading to fin with 55° sweepback. Very slight wing anhedral. Airbrakes each side of rear fuselage, forward of tailplane. All-moving horizontal tail surfaces. Large main wing fence on each side. Single mainwheels retract inward into centre section and single nosewheel retracts forward. Brake-chute housing between base of rudder and tailpipe. Rearward-hinged canopy.

Variants: Su-22U 'Fitter-E' — tandem two-seat trainer, developed from Su-17M-2, with Tumansky engine; Su-22 'Fitter-F' — export Su-17M-2; Su-22UM-3K 'Fitter-G' — export Su-17UM-3; Su-22M-3 'Fitter-J' — as

Su-17M-3 with R-29 engine; Su-22M-4 'Fitter-K' — as Su-17M-4, with AL-21F-3 engine.

Below: A Sukhoi Su-22M-4K 'Fitter' of the Czech AF. *PRM*

Sukhoi Su-25 'Frog foot'

Single-seat close support aircraft and two-seat trainer
Basic data for Su-25K 'Frogfoot-A'
Powerplant: Two Soyuz/Tumansky R-195 turbojets of 9,921lb st (44.18kN)
Span: 47ft 1½in (14.36m)
Length: 50ft 11½in (15.53m)
Max speed: 606mph (975km/h)
Armament: One twin-barrel AO-17A 30mm gun in bottom of front fuselage on port side. Eight large pylons under wings for 9,700lb of air-to-ground weapons — including UB-32A or B-8M1 rocket pods, S-25 guided rockets, Kh-23/25/29 air-to-surface missiles, laser-guided bombs. Can be fitted with SPPU-22 pods, each containing a 23mm GSh-23 gun, with twin barrels, that can pivot downward for attacking ground targets. Two small outboard pylons for R-3S or R-60 air-to-air self-defence missiles.
First aircraft flown: 22 February 1975
Entered service: February 1981
Current service: With the Russian armed forces; also in Afghanistan, Angola, Belarus, Bulgaria, Czech Republic, Georgia, Hungary, Iraq, Kazakhstan, North Korea, Peru, Slovakia and Ukraine.
Recognition: Shoulder-mounted wings with 20° sweepback and anhedral from roots. Dog-tooth wing leading-edge. Wingtip pods each split at rear to form airbrakes that project above and below pod when extended. Pitot on port side of nose.

Conventional tail unit. Variable incidence tailplane, with slight dihedral. Widely separated engines in long nacelles at wing roots. Slab sided fuselage and small cockpit. Mainwheels retract to lie horizontally in bottom of engine air intake trunks. Radar-warning system antenna above fuselage tail cone.

Variants: Su-25 'Frogfoot-A' — single-seat close support aircraft of which Su-25K is the export version; Su-25UB 'Frogfoot-B' — tandem two-seat operational conversion and weapons trainer; Su-25UT — as UB, but without weapons; Su-25UTG — as UT, with added arrester hook under tail; Su-39 — anti-tank aircraft, with rear cockpit faired over and internal space used to house new avionics.

Below: The Sukhoi Su-25K 'Frogfoot' single-seat close support aircraft. *PRM*

Sukhoi Su-27/30/32/33 'Flanker'

Single-seat long-range air superiority fighter

Basic data for Su-27 'Flanker-B'

Powerplant: Two Saturn/Lyulka AL-31F turbofans of 16,755lb st (74.53kN) and 27,558lb st (122.59kN) with afterburner

Span: 48ft 3in (14.70m)

Length: 72ft 0in (21.94m) without probe

Max speed: 1,336mph (2,150km/h)

Armament: 10 or 12 weapons pylons with maximum ordnance of 17,636lb (8,000kg). Single-barrel 30mm GSh-301 cannon. Weapons include up to 10 AAMs comprising semi-active radar-guided R-27Rs (AA-10A 'Alamo-A'), IR-guided R-27Ts (AA-10B 'Alamo-B'), semi-active radar-guided R-27ERs (AA-10C 'Alamo-C'), IR-guided R-27ETs (AA-10D 'Alamo-D'), R-73s (AA-11 'Archer') and R-60s (AA-8 'Aphid').

First aircraft flown: 20 May 1977 (T-10 prototype); 20 April 1981 (Su-27)

Entered service: December 1984 (Su-27)

Current service: With the Russian armed forces plus China, India, Kazakhstan, Syria and Ukraine.

Recognition: A long nose with a raised cockpit canopy. Large moderately swept wing with square tips. Underwing wedge-shaped air intakes close into the fuselage. Widely spaced twin fins either side of the rear fuselage. Pointed rear fuselage cone extending beyond the engine nozzles. Twin ventral fins.

Variants: Su-27 'Flanker-B' is the standard production version, and Su-27P 'Flanker-B' the basic defence version of the same aircraft; Su-27UB 'Flanker-C' — a two-seat combat trainer; Su-27SK — export version of single-seat Su-27s; the Su-30 (Su-27PU) — a two-seat long-range interceptor/multi-role fighter derivative, now in service with the Russian air defence forces and offered for export as the Su-30MK, with thrust vectoring as an option; Su-32FN (Su-27IB) is a two-seat strike derivative, designed as an Su-24 'Fencer' replacement; Su-33 (Su-27K) 'Flanker-D' — the shipborne fighter, ordered by Russian Naval Aviation; Su-35 (Su-27M) with canard foreplanes is an advanced air-superiority fighter with ground attack capability; Su-37 — similar to the Su-35, but using thrust vectoring for enhanced manoeuvrability.

Below: **A single-seat Sukhoi Su-27 'Flanker B' long-range air-defence fighter.** *PRM*

Transall C-160

Twin-turboprop tactical transport
Basic data for Transall C-160F
Powerplant: Two Rolls-Royce Tyne Rty20 Mk 22 turboprops of 6,100eshp (4,550kW)
Span: 131ft 3in (40.00m)
Length: 106ft 4in (32.41m)
Max speed: 318mph (513km/h)
Accommodation: Crew of three with a maximum payload of 35,273lb (16,000kg), or up to 93 troops.
First aircraft flown: 25 February 1963
Entered service: May 1968
Current service: With the French, German, Indonesian, South African and Turkish air forces.
Recognition: Circular fuselage section with a short nose forward of the flightdeck. High-set slightly-tapered wings with dihedral in the outer section. Sharply upswept rear fuselage providing a rear access ramp for loading and parachuting. Large angular fin and rudder with the tailplane extending beyond the rear fuselage, below the

rudder. A large dorsal extension of the fin reaches forward to a point above the side cabin doors. The main undercarriage retracts into a fuselage fairing below the wing.
Variants: Built by the Franco-German Transport Allianz consortium, initial deliveries were of C-160Ds to the German AF and C-160Fs to the French AF. The latter are now in the process of being modified to C-160R status, and new-production C-160NGs were (in the late 1970s/early 1980s) added to the French fleet with greater fuel capacity and more modern avionics. Two C-160G GABRIEL modifications are used for ELINT and jamming, while four C-160H ASTARTE conversions have special equipment for communications with France's nuclear submarines. Other Transall operators are Turkey (with surplus German aircraft delivered in the early 1970s) and Indonesia, while South Africa has retired its C-160Z fleet.

Below: **Transall C-160Ds are in service with the French, German and Turkish Air Forces.** *PRM*

Tupolev Tu-95/142 'Bear'

Four-turboprop long-range bomber and ASW aircraft
Basic data for Tu-95MS 'Bear-H'
Powerplant: Four KKBM Kuznetsov NK-12MV turboprops of 14,795eshp (11,033kW)
Span: 167ft 8in (51.10m)

Length: 162ft 5in (49.50m)
Max speed: 575mph (925km/h)
Armament: The Tu-95MS can carry six RK-55 (AS-15 'Kent') cruise missiles in its internal weapons bay, and also 10 more on underwing pylons on later production aircraft. Rear turret

contains a twin-barrelled GSh-23L cannon. Earlier 'Bears' could be equipped with such as the Kh-20 (AS-3 'Kangaroo') and Kh-22 (AS-4 'Kitchen') missiles. Maritime Tu-142s have a maximum weapons load of some 25,000lb (11,340kg), and can operate with torpedoes and depth bombs.

First aircraft flown: 12 November 1952 (Tu-95); 1983 (Tu-95MS)
Entered service: April 1956 (Tu-95M)
Current service: No Tu-95s were exported, all being in Russian service and mostly with Long-Range Aviation though some have passed to Belarus and Ukraine; Tu-142s are used by Russian Naval Aviation and the Indian Navy.
Recognition: Long, thin fuselage of tubular appearance with a shoulder-mounted swept wing. Tall, angular fin and rudder with streamlined pods at the fin tip on Tu-142, less pronounced on the Tu-95MS. Four eight-bladed contra-rotating propellers, and extended inboard engine nacelles house the rearward-retracting main undercarriage

legs. Pointed nose, with small cockpit canopy above. Tu-95MS has deeper, shorter nose radome while Tu-142 has glazed nose. All current versions have a refuelling probe.

Variants: Tu-95M 'Bear-A' was first bomber production version; Tu-95K-22 'Bear-G' — bomber and ELINT conversion; Tu-95RT 'Bear-D' — maritime reconnaissance conversion; Tu-95MR 'Bear-E' is the strategic reconnaissance conversion of the Tu-95M. From 1982 onwards, Tupolev reopened the production line to build the Tu-95MS 'Bear-H', with various features of the naval Tu-142 including the NK-12MV turboprops, radar and weapon changes. Tu-142 'Bear-F' — first dedicated MR/ASW version; Tu-142M — improved variant, with lengthened nose and MAD boom fitted to fin tip; Tu-142MR 'Bear-J' — with VLF communications avionics, operates as communications relay aircraft; Tu-142M-3 'Bear-F' — final production version, last built in 1992.

Below: A Tupolev Tu-95 'Bear' operated by Russia's Long-Range Aviation. *PRM*

107

Westland Wessex

Medium-lift utility helicopter
Basic data for Wessex HC2

Powerplant: Two Rolls-Royce Gnome 112/113 coupled turbines of 1,550eshp (1,156kW)

Rotor diameter: 56ft 0in (17.07m)

Length: 48ft 4½in (14.74m)

Max speed: 132mph (212km/h)

Accommodation: Crew of two and 16 troops

First aircraft flown: 17 May 1957 (HAS1); 18 January 1962 (HC2)

Entered service: July 1961 (HAS1); January 1964 (HC2)

Current service: With the RAF and the Uruguay Air Force.

Recognition: Engines located in the nose with a front air intake and exhaust pipes below the cockpit, which is situated above the passenger cabin. Fuselage tapers gradually to the tailfin. Four-blade main rotor located behind and above the cockpit. Fixed undercarriage with large mainwheels either side of the cabin; tailwheel below the rear fuselage. Four-blade tail rotor on the port side of the fin.

Variants: The original Sikorsky S-58/CH-34 was piston-engined; like the subsequent H-34, few examples remain airworthy. All of the subsequent Westland-built Wessex versions have been retired except for the HC2, which still serves in limited numbers with the RAF and the Uruguayan Air Force, which received retired RAF Wessex in 1997 and 1998.

Below: A Westland WS58 Wessex HC2 helicopter operating with the RAF in Cyprus. *PRM*

Aérospatiale (Fouga) CM170 Magister
Twin-turbojet trainer/light-attack aircraft
Powerplant: Two Turboméca Marboré IIA turbojets of
882lb st (3.92kN)
Span: 37ft 5in (11.40m)
Length: 33ft 0in (10.06m)
Current service: With the air forces of Algeria,
Bangladesh, Belgium, Cameroon, Eire, El Salvador,
France, Gabon, Israel, Morocco, Senegambia and Togo.
Variants: The CM170 Magister now serves in dwindling
numbers, used for various training, liaison and light
attack duties. Israel operates its modernised aircraft as
the Tzukit (meaning Thrush); the CM175 Zéphyr is now
retired from French Navy service.

Above: **A small number of CM170 Magisters
remain in service with the Irish Air Corps.**
PRM

Airbus A310-300
Twin-engined VIP/strategic transport
Powerplant: Two Pratt & Whitney JT9D-7RR4D1
turbofans of 48,000lb st (213.76kN) or General Electric
CF6-80A3 turbofans of 50,000lb st (222.6kN)
Span: 144ft 0in (43.89m)
Length: 153ft 1in (46.66m)
Current service: With Belgium, the Canadian Forces
(designated CC-150 Polaris), France, Germany and
Thailand.
Variants: The French AF version has a large cargo door
and underwing hose reel pods; the A310-200 is the basic
passenger version; A310-200C is the convertible version of
the -200; A310-200F is the freighter version; A310-300 is the
extended range version.

Above: **A military derivative of the Airbus
A310-300 airliner, this CC-100 Polaris is
flown by the Canadian Armed Forces.** *APM*

Antonov An-12 'Cub'
**Four-turboprop transport and electronic
warfare aircraft**
Basic data for An-12BP
Powerplant: Four Ivchenko Progress AI-20K
turboprops of 4,000eshp (2,983kW)
Span: 124ft 9in (38.028m)
Length: 108ft 7½in (33.11m)
Current service: Used by the Russian armed forces and in
Egypt, Ethiopia, Iraq, Slovakia, Ukraine and Sri Lanka. Also
as the Yunshuji-8 in China and Sri Lanka.
Variants: An-12, An-12A, An-12B and An-12BK 'Cub-A'
— all transport versions; An-12BPL — fixed ski
undercarriage; An-12PS — search and rescue derivative;
An-12BK-VKP Zebra — airborne command post; An-12PP
and An-12PPS — electronic warfare versions. Still in
production in China as the Y-8.

Above: **Antonov An-12 'Cub' of the Slovak
Air Force.** *PRM*

Antonov An-32 'Cline'
Twin-turboprop short/medium-range transport

Powerplant: Two ZMKB Progress AI-20D Series 5 turboprops of 5,042eshp (3,760kW)
Span: 95ft 9½in (29.20m)
Length: 78ft ¼in (23.78m)
Current service: With the Russian armed forces and government agencies; also used by Afghanistan, Bangladesh, India, Peru and Ukraine.
Variants: An-32 — standard version; An-32B — introduced 1993 with higher payload; An-32P (Pozharnyi) Firekiller is the fire-fighting version, also used for 'weather adjustment' purposes.

Above: This Antonov An-32 'Cline' twin-turboprop transport serves with the Ukrainian Air Force. *Gordon Bartley*

Antonov An-72/74 'Coaler'
Twin-turbofan STOL transport and maritime patrol aircraft

Powerplant: Two ZMKB Progress D-36 high bypass ratio turbofans of 14,330lb st (63.81kN)
Span: 140ft 7½in (31.89m)
Length: 92ft 1¼in (28.07m)
Current service: Russian air forces and Border Guards; also with Iran and Ukraine.
Variants: An-72 'Coaler-B' is the standard military version; An-72P is the maritime patrol aircraft, as used by the Russian Border Guards with a 23mm gun pod and rocket pack under wings; An-72S — a VIP transport; An-74-200 'Coaler-B' is for all-weather operations in the Arctic; An-74T-200 and An-74TK-200 — additional cargo versions; An-747-100 and TK-100 have a navigator station.

Above: The Antonov An-74 'Coaler' is in limited service as a STOL transport. *PRM*

Antonov An-124 Ruslan/'Condor'
Four-turbofan very heavy strategic transport

Powerplant: Four ZMKB Progress D-18T turbofans of 51,587lb st (229.47kN)
Span: 240ft 5¾in (73.30m)
Length: 226ft 8½in (69.10m)
Current service: With the Russian AF — most An-124s carry Aeroflot markings but these commonly perform military tasks, a small number having military liveries.
Variants: Only one basic version of the An-124 — however, it was developed into the six-engined, twin-finned An-225 Mriya/'Cossack', the world's largest and heaviest aircraft but which has not entered production.

Above: Antonov An-124 Ruslan, the Soviet Air Force's big transport aircraft, is also chartered to civil airlines. *PRM*

Beech T-34C Turbo Mentor
Two-seat primary/basic trainer
Powerplant: One Pratt & Whitney PT6A-25
turboprop of 715eshp (533kW)
Span: 33ft 5½in (10.20m)
Length: 28ft 9in (8.75m)
Current service: With the US Navy, and the
air forces of Argentina, Ecuador, Gabon,
Indonesia, Morocco, Peru, Taiwan and
Uruguay.

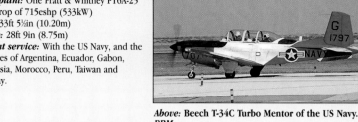

Above: Beech T-34C Turbo Mentor of the US Navy.
PRM

Beechcraft T-1A Jayhawk
Twin-turbofan military trainer
Powerplant: Two Pratt & Whitney Canada
JT15D-5 turbofans of 2,900lb st (12.91kN)
Span: 43ft 6in (13.25m)
Length: 48ft 5in (14.75m)
Current service: T-1A Jayhawk with USAF
since 1992. 400T with Japanese Air Self-
Defence Force (JASDF) since 1996, as a
transport aircrew trainer.
Variants: Beechjet 400 — initial production
version, based on the Mitsubishi MU-300
Diamond; Beechjet 400T/T-1A Jayhawk for
the US Air Force requirement for a Tanker
Transport/Training System (TTTS) aircraft — a
specialised undergraduate pilot training
system — which is based on the improved
Beechjet 400A. The 180th and last T-1A was
delivered in 1997.

Above: Beechcraft T-1A Jayhawks have been used
with the USAF since 1992 for tanker and transport
crew training. *PRM*

Boeing 727/C-22
**Three-turbojet long-range
passenger/VIP transport**
Basic data for 727-200/C-22C
Powerplant: Three Pratt & Whitney JT8D-9A
turbofans of 14,500lb st (64.5kN)
Span: 108ft 0in (32.92m)
Length: 136ft 2in (41.51m)
Current service: With the US ANG, and the
air forces of Belgium, Mexico and New
Zealand.
Variants: USAF derivatives are the C-22B
(ex-airline 727-100s, now staff transports for
the ANG Bureau) and C-22C (a former
Singapore Airlines 727-200, used by Central
Command), while other operators use a
mixture of -100 and -200 examples.

Above: Boeing 727s remain in service as a military
transport with four air arms. *PRM*

Boeing 737/CT-43A
Twin-turbofan navigation trainer/maritime surveillance/VIP transport
Basic data for 737-200/CT-43A
Powerplant: Two Pratt & Whitney JT8D-9A turbofans of 14,500lb st (64.5kN)
Span: 93ft 0in (28.54m)
Length: 100ft 0in (30.50m)
Current service: With the USAF, and also Brazil, India, Indonesia, Mexico, Niger, Thailand, South Korea and Venezuela.
Variants: The USAF operates the 737-200 as the CT-43A, used as staff transports and navigation

Above: The Boeing 737-200 serves with the USAF as the CT-43A. *PRM*

trainers. Indonesia flies the 737-200 Surveiller on maritime patrol duties, equipped with side-looking radar, while other operators use civilian transport versions.

British Aerospace Jetstream
Twin-turboprop light transport/multi-engine trainer
Basic data for Jetstream T1/T2
Powerplant: Two Turboméca Astazou XVID turboprops of 913eshp (681kW)
Span: 52ft 0in (15.85m)
Length: 47ft 2in (14.37m)
Current service: RAF, RN and Royal Saudi Air Force.
Variants: The Jetstream T1, used by the RAF as multi-engine trainers and T2, the RN's observer trainer were built by Handley Page/Scottish Aviation; the later BAe Jetstream 31 development powered by the TPE331 engine is flown by the RN as the T3, and the Royal Saudi AF.

Above: Jetstream T1/T2s are powered by the Turboméca Astazou turboprop. *PRM*

Canadair CL600/601 Challenger
Twin-turbofan military VIP transport, flight inspection/calibration and electronic warfare training aircraft.
Powerplant: CL600 — two Avco Lycoming ALF-502L turbofans of 7,500lb st (33.6kN); CL601 — two General Electric CF34-3A turbofans of 9,140lb st (40.66kN)
Span: 64ft 4in (19.61m)
Length: 68ft 5in (20.85m)
Current service: With the Canadian Forces, plus the air forces of China, Croatia, Germany and Malaysia.
Variants: The CL600 was replaced by the CL601, which has winglets and the CF34 engines; some earlier aircraft have been thus modified since

Above: A Canadair CL601-1 Challenger flown by the German Air Force. *PRM*

(designated CL600S), including those of Canada whose aircraft are a mixture of CC-144 transports and CE-144 electronic support/training aircraft. Malaysia's Challengers are CL600s, and the Chinese, Croatian and German AF VIP transports are CL601s. A long-range version, the CL604, was introduced in 1996.

Cessna A-37/T-37

Twin-turbojet light two-seat attack aircraft and basic trainer

Basic data for T-37B

Powerplant: Two Teledyne Continental J69-T-25 turbojets of 1,025lb st (4.56kN)
Span: 33ft 9¼in (10.30m)
Length: 29ft 3in (8.92m)
Current service: T-37 — with the USAF plus Chile, Colombia, Greece, Morocco, Pakistan, Peru, Thailand and Turkey; A-37 — Chile, Ecuador, El Salvador, Guatemala, Honduras, South Korea and Thailand.
Variants: The initial T-37A and B, together with the export T-37C, were all externally similar. The A-37 has a more powerful J85-GE-17A engine, and

Above: **Cessna T-37s are still used by the USAF for basic jet training.** *PRM*

can be distinguished by its refuelling probe, underwing hardpoints and fuselage aerials. USAF T-37s have been undergoing a service life-extension programme (SLEP), engineered by the Sabreliner Corporation, prior to their replacement by the Beech T-6 under the JPATS programme.

Dassault Falcon 10MER

Twin-turbofan transport/systems trainer

Powerplant: Two Garrett AiResearch TFE 731-2 turbofans of 3,230lb st (14.38kN)
Span: 42ft 11in (13.08m)
Length: 45ft 5in (13.85m)
Current service: With the French Navy.
Variants: The 10MER is unique to the French Navy, being used for a variety of duties including radar training, transport/liaison and target facilities work. The aircraft can carry such as ECM jammer pods and chaff dispensers on wingtip pylons.

Above: **Dassault Falcon 10MER operated by the French Navy as a systems trainer.** *PRM*

Dassault Mirage IV

Twin-turbojet reconnaissance/nuclear strike aircraft

Basic data for Mirage IVP

Powerplant: Two SNECMA Atar 9K-50 turbojets of 11,023lb st (49.03kN) dry and 15,873lb st (70.61kN) with afterburner
Span: 38ft 10½in (11.85m)
Length: 77ft 1in (23.50m)
Current service: With the French AF only.
Variants: Original Mirage IVA designed to meet the French AF's nuclear strike aircraft requirement; 19 were converted in the late 1980s to Mirage IVP standard, able to carry the Aérospatiale ASMP. Now only five are operational at any one time and are only used for reconnaissance tasks, the Mirage 2000N having replaced the IVP in the nuclear role.

Above: **A few Mirage IVAs remain in service with the French Air Force.** *PRM*

De Havilland Canada DHC-5 Buffalo
Twin-turboprop STOL utility transport
Basic data for DHC-5A
Powerplant: Two General Electric CT64-820-1 turboprops of 3,055eshp (2,278kW)
Span: 96ft 0in (29.26m)
Length: 79ft 0in (24.08m)
Current service: In Abu Dhabi, Brazil, Cameroon, Canada, Democratic Republic of Congo, Ecuador, Indonesia, Kenya, Mauritania, Mexico, Sudan, Tanzania, Togo and Zambia.
Variants: The Canadian Forces operate the aircraft under the CC-115 designation, using them for SAR tasks; Brazilian machines are named C-115B. The DHC-5D, with CT64-820-4 engines, entered production in 1974 (the DHC-5B and C were not built), the first customer being Egypt.

Above: **De Havilland Canada DHC-5 Buffalo, operated here by the Canadian Armed Forces.** *PRM*

De Havilland Canada DHC-6 Twin Otter
Twin-turboprop utility transport
Basic data for Series 300
Powerplant: Two Pratt & Whitney PT6A-27 turboprops of 620eshp (462kW)
Span: 65ft 0in (19.81m)
Length: 51ft 9in (15.77m)
Current service: With the air arms of Argentina, Benin, Canada, Chile, Ecuador, Ethiopia, France, Haiti, Nepal, Norway, Panama, Paraguay, Peru, Sudan, Uganda and the US Army.
Variants: First main production version was the Series 100 with PT6A-20 engines (sold to the Canadian Forces and operated as the CC-138), developed into the Series 200 equipped with a lengthened nose and then the PT6A-27-powered Series 300. The US Army aircraft are known as UV-18s. Twin Otters can be fitted with skis or floats.

Above: **De Havilland Canada DHC-6 Twin Otters are widely used as STOL multi-role transports**. *PRM*

Dornier Do28D Skyservant
Twin piston-engined utility transport
Basic data for Do28D-1
Powerplant: Two Textron Lycoming IGSO-540 piston engines of 380hp (283kW)
Span: 50ft 10¼in (15.50m)
Length: 39ft 4½in (12.0m)
Current service: In Benin, Cameroon, Croatia, Greece, Israel, Kenya, Malawi, Morocco, Niger, Nigeria, Turkey and Zambia.
Variants: First production version was the Do28D-1, followed by the Do28D-2 with a lengthened fuselage — the latter was used particularly by the German AF and Navy, but has now been retired by both. The Model 128 was an updated derivative which did not see widespread military service.

Above: **Dornier Do28D Skyservants are now only operated by smaller air arms in third world countries.** *PRM*

Dornier 228
Twin-turboprop multi-purpose transport
Basic data for 228-200
Powerplant: Two Garrett TPE331-5-252D
turboprops of 715eshp (533kW)
Span: 55ft 8in (16.97m)
Length: 49ft 4in (15.04m)
Current service: German Navy and AF; also in
Cape Verde, India, Malawi, Niger, Nigeria and
Thailand.
Variants: The 228-100 and 228-200 are identical,
save for the latter's slightly longer fuselage. India
is the largest military operator, mostly maritime
patrol versions with the Navy and Coast Guard —
these are licence-built by HAL. The German Navy
also uses the 228-200 for maritime pollution control.

Above: Four Dornier 228s are operated by the
German Navy. *PRM*

Embraer EMB121 Xingu
**Twin-turboprop VIP/light military
transport**
Basic data for Xingu II
Powerplant: Two Pratt & Whitney PT6A-42
turboprops of 850eshp (635kW)
Span: 48ft 8in (14.83m)
Length: 44ft 1in (13.44m)
Current service: With the Brazilian AF, French AF
and French Navy.
Variants: The nine Brazilian AF aircraft (all VIP
transports, locally designated VU-9 and EC-9) are
all Xingu Is; French examples are Xingu IIs, either
EMB121AA for the French AF, or EMB121AN in
Navy service.

Above: Embraer EMB-121 Xingu of the French
Navy. *DJM*

Fairchild Metro/C-26
Twin-turboprop special missions and light transport aircraft
Basic data for Metro III/C-26
Powerplant: Two Garrett TPE331-121UAR
turboprops of 1,120eshp (835kW)
Span: 57ft 0in (17.37m)
Length: 59ft 5in (18.10m)
Current service: With the US ANG, and also in
Argentina, Belgium, Mexico, Sweden and Thailand.
Variants: The US ANG operates C-26A/B versions
of the Metro III as operational support aircraft,
plus a UC-26C for anti-drug missions (equipped
with FLIR and APG-66 radar). Various
Metros/Merlins have also been sold to other air arms.
Fairchild has also developed the MMSA (Multi-
Mission Surveillance Aircraft), which is rapidly
convertible to different special mission roles with
its systems pod on the fuselage centreline.

Above: Fairchild C-26 Metro III of the US Air
National Guard. *APM*

Gates Learjet/C-21
Twin-turbofan light utility/VIP transport
Basic data for Learjet 35A/C-21A
Powerplant: Two Garrett AiResearch TFE731-2-2B turbofans of 3,500lb st (15.6kN)
Span: 39ft 4in (12.04m)
Length: 48ft 8in (14.83m)
Current service: Used by the USAF as the C-21A; also in service with the air arms of Argentina, Bolivia, Brazil, Chile, Ecuador, Finland, Japan, Mexico, Oman, Peru, Saudi Arabia, Switzerland, Thailand and Venezuela.
Variants: Learjet 24/25 has General Electric CJ610 turbojets and is smaller. Model

Above: **Learjets are widely used as VIP jet transports.** *PRM*

35A/36A, the USAF's C-21, has been developed for reconnaissance, ECM training, target-towing and radar surveillance as well as transport duties.

Grob G115
Two-seat light training aircraft
Powerplant: One Textron Lycoming 0-320-D1A piston engine of 160hp (119.3kW)
Span: 32ft 9¾in (10.0m)
Length: 24ft 5in (7.44m)
Current service: Royal Navy (G115D-2, operated by Short Bros under the name Heron), UAE Air Force (G115T).
Variants: G115C — the utility version, not intended for aerobatic training; G115D — an aerobatic aircraft; G115T — another aerobatic version with a retractable undercarriage; G115 Bavarian — civil export version for Florida.

Above: **This Grob G115 Heron is used for flying grading under contract to the Royal Navy.** *PRM*

Grumman C-2A Greyhound
Twin-turboprop carrier on-board delivery aircraft
Powerplant: Two Allison T56-A-427 turboprops of 4,910eshp (3,665kW)
Span: 80ft 7in (24.56m)
Length: 56ft 8in (17.27m)
Current service: US Navy for carrier on-board delivery (COD) and communications.
Variants: Only the C-2A.

Above: **The C-2A Greyhound is used by the US Navy for carrier on-board delivery (COD) and light transport duties.** *PRM*

Gulfstream Aviation Gulfstream II/III

Twin-turbofan VIP transport and reconnaissance aircraft

Basic data for Gulfstream III

Powerplant: Two Rolls-Royce Spey turbofans of 11,400lb st (51.1kN)
Span: 77ft 10in (23.72m)
Length: 83ft 1in (25.32m)
Current service: With the US forces and in Croatia, Denmark, India, Italy, Mexico, Morocco, Saudi Arabia and Venezuela.
Variants: The Gulfstream II is a jet-powered development of the original turboprop Gulfstream I,

Above: **Gulfstream IIIs have distinctive drag-reducing winglets.** *PRM*

while the Gulfstream III has a revised wing of greater span with drag-reducing winglets. In US service, as a military VIP transport, it is designated C-20. The Gulfstream III was used as the basis for the SRA-1 (Surveillance and Reconnaissance Aircraft) which was built in a variety of ELINT, reconnaissance and maritime patrol configurations.

Gulfstream Aerospace Gulfstream IV/IV-SP

Twin-turbofan VIP and utility transport and multi-role surveillance aircraft

Powerplant: Two Rolls-Royce Tay Mk 611-8 turbofans of 13,850lb st (61.6kN)
Span: 77ft 10in (23.72m)
Length: 88ft 4in (26.92m)
Current service: Eire, Japan, Netherlands, Sweden, Turkey and USA.
Variants: The Gulfstream IV was the initial version, replaced by the IV-SP in September 1992. Gulfstream IV-B — a projected longer-range model; Gulfstream IV-MPA — a multi-purpose aircraft. C-20F — the US Army version; C-20G — for the US Navy and

Above: **Gulfstream Aerospace Gulfstream IVs operated by the USAF as the C-20H.** *PRM*

USMC; C-20H — the USAF variant. The SRA-4 is available in a variety of special missions configurations, including electronic warfare support, ASW and maritime patrol (can be armed with two anti-shipping missiles on two underwing hardpoints), ELINT and medical evacuation.

Ilyushin Il-38 'May'

Four-turboprop maritime patrol and ASW aircraft

Powerplant: Four ZMKB Progress (Ivchenko) A1-20M turboprops of 4,190eshp (3,125kW)
Span: 122ft 9in (37.42m)
Length: 129ft 10in (36.90m)
Current service: Russian Naval Aviation and India.
Variants: Il-38 is the military adaptation of the Il-18 airliner, and the tail contains a MAD.
A search radar is housed in a bulged radome under the forward fuselage. Two internal weapons bays — one forward and one rear of the wing.

Above: **Russian Naval Aviation uses the Ilyushin Il-38 'May' as a turboprop maritime patrol and ASW aircraft.** *APM*

Let L-410 Turbolet
Twin-turboprop general purpose light utility transport
Basic data for L-410UVP
Powerplant: Two Motorlet M601E turboprops of 750eshp (559kW)
Span: 65ft 6½in (19.98m) over tip tanks; 63ft 11in (19.48m) excluding tip tanks
Length: 47ft 4in (14.42m)
Current service: Air forces of Bulgaria, Czech Republic, Germany, Hungary, Latvia, Libya, Lithuania, Russia, Slovakia and Slovenia.
Variants: L-410UVP was the original version, L-410UVP-E is the post-1984 and current production version; L-420, introduced 1993, is an improved version with M601F engine and Western avionics.

Above: Let L-410 Turbolets are operated as a light utility transport by several European air forces. *PRM*

Lockheed (Canadair) T-33/CT-133 Silver Star
Single-turbojet two-seat trainer
Powerplant: One Rolls-Royce Nene 10 turbojet of 5,100lb st (22.7kN)
Span: 38ft 10in (11.85m)
Length: 37ft 9in (11.5lm)
Current service: With the Canadian Forces and in Bolivia, Ecuador, Greece, Iran, Japan, Mexico, Pakistan, South Korea, Thailand, Turkey and Uruguay.
Variants: The T-33, as built by Lockheed (and in Japan by Kawasaki) had an Allison J33 turbojet. Canadair produced it with the Nene engine as the T-33AN/CT-133 Silver Star.

Above: Lockheed/Canadair T-33 Silver Star of the Canadian Forces. *PRM*

LTV F-8 Crusader
Single-turbojet single-seat carrier-borne fighter
Basic data for F-8P
Powerplant: One Pratt & Whitney J57-P-20-A turbojet of 10,700lb st (47.6kN) dry and 18,000lb st (80.1kN) with afterburner
Span: 35ft 8in (10.87m)
Length: 54ft 6in (16.61m)
Current service: With the French Navy.
Variants: Now that all Crusaders have been retired by the US Navy and Marine Corps, and the Philippines, the only examples left in service anywhere are the French Navy's long-serving F-8Ps. These aircraft have recently

Above: LTV's F-8 Crusader remains operational as a carrier-borne fighter with the French Navy. *PRM*

been upgraded with a new missile warning system and better navigation equipment — prior to this, they were designated F-8E(FN). They will remain in use until the Rafale M's arrival.

Mikoyan MiG-31 'Foxhound'

Two-seat twin-engined strategic interceptor

Basic data for MiG-31 'Foxhound-A'
Powerplant: Two Aviadvigatel D-30F6 turbofans of 34,170lb st (152.17kN) with afterburner
Span: 44ft 2in (13.46m)
Length: 74ft 5¼in (22.69m)
Current service: With the Russian air forces.
Variants: MiG-31 'Foxhound-A' is the original version; MiG-31M 'Foxhound-B' is an improved interceptor with upgraded engines and avionics, but unlikely to see service; MiG-31D is similar to the 'M' but with the original radar.

Above: A Russian Air Force MiG-31 'Foxhound' twin-turbofan interceptor fighter. *PRM*

Mil Mi-28 'Havoc'

Two-seat twin-turbine combat helicopter

Powerplant: Two Klimov TV3-117 VM turboshafts of 2,070eshp (1,546.6kW)
Rotor diameter: 56ft 5in (17.20m)
Fuselage length: 55ft 10in (17.01m)
Current service: Only with the Russian Army.
Variants: Mi-28 'Havoc' is the standard version. Mi-28N is the all-weather day and night variant and has mast-mounted millimetric-wave radar, which entered service in 1997. Projected versions for naval amphibious assault support and air-to-air missions have been announced.

Above: The Mil Mi-28N 'Havoc' all-weather day and night variant combat helicopter now in service with the Russian Army. *PRM*

Northrop Grumman E-8 J-Stars

Four-engined long-range radar and battlefield reconnaissance aircraft

Basic data for E-8C
Powerplant: Four Pratt & Whitney JT8D-3B turbofans of 18,000lb st (80.16kN)
Span: 145ft 9in (44.42m)
Length: 152ft 11in (44.61m)
Current service: Production deliveries of re-manufactured ex-commercial Boeing 707-300 airframes began in 1996, to be operated by the USAF on behalf of the US Army. 18 production E-8C conversions are to be delivered up to March 2001.

Above: Operated by the USAF on behalf of the US Army, the Northrop Grumman E-8C J-Stars is used for battlefield reconnaissance. *APM*

Variants: E-8A — two development aircraft, which flew 49 missions during Operation Desert Storm in 1991 (to be upgraded to E-8C standard); E-8B — original proposed production version, but not proceeded with; E-8C — current production version.

Piaggio PD-808
Twin-turbojet light utility and ECM aircraft

Powerplant: Two Rolls-Royce Viper turbojets of 3,360lb st (14.96kN).

Span: 43ft 3½in (12.20m)

Length: 42ft 2in (12.85m)

Current service: Italian AF for VIP transport, communications, calibration duties and electronic warfare.

Variants: Still in service are the standard transport PD-808TA, the PD-808GE for EW training and the PD-808RM navaid/airways checker.

Above: **The Piaggio PD-808 continues in service with the Italian Air Force.** *PRM*

Pilatus PC-6 Turbo Porter
Single-turboprop STOL utility transport
Basic data for PC-6/B2-H4

Powerplant: One Pratt & Whitney PT6A-27 turboprop of 550eshp (410kW)

Span: 52ft 1in (15.87m)

Length: 36ft 1in (11.0m)

Current service: With the Swiss AF; also in Angola, Argentina, Australia, Austria, Bolivia, Chad, Colombia, Dubai, Ecuador, France, Indonesia, Iran, Myanmar, Oman, Peru and Sudan.

Variants: Developed from the piston-engined PC-6 Porter, different versions of the Turbo Porter denote different engine options: PC-6/A

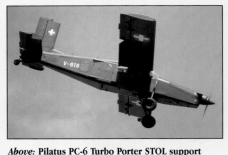

Above: **Pilatus PC-6 Turbo Porter STOL support aircraft.** *APM*

— Turboméca Astazou; PC-6/B — PT6A; PC-6/C — Garrett TPE331. The most recent PC-6/B2-H4 has a greater payload and upturned wingtips.

Slingsby T67M/T-3A Firefly
Single piston-engined two-seat military basic trainer
Basic data for T67M-260/T-3A

Powerplant: One Textron Lycoming AEIO-540-D4A5 piston engine of 260hp (193.9kW)

Span: 34ft 9in (10.59m)

Length: 23ft 10in (7.55m)

Current service: The RAF, RN and AAC use various versions for elementary flying training, operated for the military by Hunting Contract Services; the air arms of the Netherlands and Norway have similar civilian arrangements. The T67M-260 serves with the USAF for its Enhanced Flight Screener (EFS) requirement.

Above: **The Slingsby T67M-260 is used by the USAF as the T-3A Firefly.** *PRM*

Variants: T67C is the low-cost aerobatic training aircraft; the T67M Mk II is the lowest-powered of the 'M' military models with an AEIO-360-D1B engine of 160hp (119.3kW). T67M-200 has an AEIO-360-A1E powerplant of 200hp (149.1kW), while the T67M-260 is used by the USAF as the T-3A Firefly.

Tupolev Tu-22M 'Backfire'

Twin-turbofan variable-geometry strategic bomber

Basic data for Tu-22M-3 'Backfire-C'

Powerplant: Two KKBM Kuznetsov NK-25 turbofans of 55,115lb st (245.2kN) with afterburner

Span: 112ft 6½in (34.3m) wings spread

Length: 129ft 11in (39.6m)

Current service: With the Russian AF and Naval Aviation, also in Belarus and Ukraine.

Variants: The initial Tu-22M-1 'Backfire-A' was a prototype for the variable-geometry wing system; first production

Above: Russia's twin-engined, variable-geometry strategic bomber, the Tupolev Tu-22M 'Backfire'. *PRM*

version was the Tu-22M-2 'Backfire-B'. This was followed by the Tu-22M-3 'Backfire-C', which has different wedge-shaped air intakes, more powerful NK-25 engines and the ability to carry three RKV-500B (AS-16 'Kickback') SRAMs, one in the internal bay and two more on underwing stations. The type has a maximum weapons load of around 26,450lb (12,000kg).

Tupolev Tu-134 'Crusty'

Two-turbofan short-to-medium range military and VIP transport

Basic data for Tu-134A

Powerplant: Two Soloviev D-30-2 turbofans of 14,490lb st (64.9kN)

Span: 95ft 2in (29.00m)

Length: 119ft 0½in (36.40m)

Current service: With the Russian armed forces; also in Angola, Bulgaria, Czech Republic and Poland, and numerous governments.

Variants: The standard Tu-134A transport version is the most numerous in military service, but two other special derivatives have been noted in Russian service — the Tu-134BSh is a bombardier trainer, with a nose-mounted Tu-22M radar and 12

Above: Tupolev Tu-134As continue in service with several former Warsaw Pact air forces. *PRM*

operators' stations in the cabin; and the outwardly-similar Tu-134UBL is used as a crew trainer for the Tu-160, which also has a reshaped nose to house the strategic bomber's radar.

Tupolev Tu-154 'Careless'
Three-turbofan medium-haul transport
Basic data for Tu-154M
Powerplant: Three Aviadvigatel D-30KU-154-II turbofans of 23,380lb st (104.0kN)
Span: 123ft 2½in (37.55m)
Length: 157ft 2in (47.90m)
Current service: In Russia, plus the air forces of the Czech Republic, Germany, North Korea, Poland and Slovakia, and with various governments.
Variants: The initial Tu-154A was superseded in production by the Tu-154B and then the improved Tu-154B-2. Later came the Tu-154M with new engines and increased passenger capacity.

Above: **Russian-built Tupolev Tu-154B long-range transport.** *PRM*

Tupolev Tu-160 'Blackjack'
Four-engined variable-geometry long-range strategic bomber
Powerplant: Four Samara/Trud NK-231 turbofans of 30,865lb st (137.4kN) dry and 55,115lb st (245.4kN) with afterburner
Span: 189ft 9in (55.70m) wings spread; 116ft 9in (35.60m) wings swept
Length: 177ft 6in (54.1m)
Current service: Only in limited numbers with Russia and Ukraine.
Variants: Tu-160 — strategic bomber version; Tu-160P — a projected escort interceptor, armed with medium and long-range AAMs, but programme is on hold;
Tu-160SK — a projected commercial version for use as a launching platform for the Burlak space vehicle.

Above: **Tupolev Tu-160 'Blackjack' long-range bomber is only in service in limited numbers with Russia and Ukraine.** *PRM*

Yakovlev Yak-40 'Codling'
Three-turbofan staff/VIP transport
Powerplant: Three ZMDB Progress AI-25 turbofans of 3,307lb st (14.71kN)
Span: 82ft 0in (25.00m)
Length: 66ft 9½in (20.36m)
Current service: With Bulgaria, Cambodia, Cuba, Ethiopia, Guinea-Bissau, Laos, Poland, Syria, Vietnam and Zambia; also used by semi-military governmental flights such as those of the Czech Republic, Russia and Slovakia.
Variants: The 32-passenger version is the sole sub-type in service.

Above: **A Yakovlev Yak-40 three-turbofan military/VIP transport aircraft.** *PRM*

SIMILAR SHAPES

Seen from the same angle many military aircraft can appear very much alike and it becomes quite difficult to tell one type from another. Here is a selection of military aircraft which are superficially similar, together with a key to their individual recognition features to help you distinguish them.

1. Boeing (McDonnell Douglas) AH-64 Apache. PRM

2. Bell AH-1 Cobra. PRM

Key Recognition Features

The Apache is a much larger helicopter and features a four-blade main rotor whereas the Cobra has only two main blades. The Apache has a four-blade tail rotor on the left side of its moderately swept fin while the Cobra's two-blade tail rotor is on the right-hand side of a more sharply swept fin.

Other Features

The Apache has a wheeled undercarriage with a tailwheel at the end of the tail boom, while the Cobra sits forward on skids. A large moving tailplane is a significant feature of the AH-64.

Key Recognition Features

The F/A-18 Hornet has a slight leading-edge sweep to the wings and straight trailing-edges, with square tips which accommodate missile pylons. It has an extended fillet stretching forward from the wing to below the cockpit. The F-15 Eagle has a more pronounced leading-edge sweep to its wings with oblique cut-off tips. The Tomcat features a more slender variable geometry swing-wing arrangement.

All three fighters have twin fins and rudders. Those on the Hornet are canted outwards at 30° and mounted well forward of the jetpipes, while the F-14 and F-15 both have vertical fins set on the rear fuselage above the jet-pipes. The all-moving tailplane of the Eagle extends significantly to the rear of the jetpipes. The Tomcat has twin ventral fins under the rear fuselage.

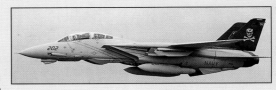

3. Grumman F-14 Tomcat. PRM

4. McDonnell Douglas F-15 Eagle. PRM

5. McDonnell Douglas F/A-18 Hornet. PRM

Other Features

The Eagle has a more pronounced high-set cockpit on the single-seat and two-seat versions whereas the Hornet and Tomcat are more conventionally shaped, the F-14 having a two-seat cockpit in all cases. The Hornet normally mounts its air-to-air missiles on wingtip rails. The Tomcat and Eagle have underwing missile pylons set well inboard close to the fuselage.

6. Lockheed Tristar. PRM

Key Recognition Features

The KC-10's third, fin-mounted engine is positioned clear of the rear fuselage and has a straight-through jet-pipe with a small extension of the fin on the top surface. The TriStar's third engine intake is moulded on to the top of the fuselage and the front of the fin. It exhausts through the fuselage tailcone aft of the tailplane.

124

8. British Aerospace Hawk. DJM

9. Dassault/Dornier Alpha Jet. DJM

Key Recognition Features

The Hawk's wing is set at the bottom of its fuselage while the Alpha Jet has a shoulder-mounted wing. The rear fuselage extends beyond the twin jet pipes of the Alpha Jet whereas the single jetpipe of the Hawk is at the extremity of the fuselage. The Hawk has a more humped appearance with a flat fuselage underside whereas the underside of the Alpha Jet is more curved.

Other Features

The Alpha Jet's nose is pointed while the Hawk's is more rounded. The Alpha Jet has a straight fin leading-edge with a dorsal spine, whereas the Hawk has a curved fin and two small ventral fins.

7. McDonnell Douglas KC-10 Extender. DJM

Other Features

The TriStar has a more shaped nose than the Extender and a broader-chord fin. The RAF's TriStar K/KC1s have an in-flight refuelling probe above the cockpit.

125

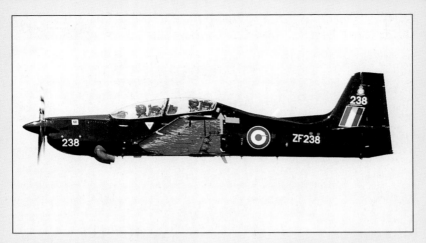

10. Shorts Tucano. DJM

11. Pilatus PC-9. PRM

Key Recognition Features

The cockpit of the Tucano is further forward and the rear seat is set higher than the PC-9's. The Tucano's fin is larger and more rounded at the top than the PC-9's and the rudder extends well to the rear of the tailplane.

Other Features

The nose of the PC-9 is longer with the twin exhaust pipes immediately to the rear of the spinner. The twin exhausts of the Tucano are further to the rear and below the fuselage.

INDEX